LIFE
IN SPORTS

IN SPORTS

A Pictorial History of Sports
from the Incomparable Archives of
America's Greatest Picture Magazine

Edited by Richard Whittingham

HARPER & ROW, PUBLISHERS, NEW YORK

CAMBRIDGE, PHILADELPHIA, SAN FRANCISCO, LONDON
MEXICO CITY, SÃO PAULO, SINGAPORE, SYDNEY

1817

ACKNOWLEDGMENTS. Special credit and thanks are extended to Gretchen Wessels, photo editor and researcher, whose contributions to this book were essential and many. Deeply appreciated are the multitudinous efforts and generous cooperation of Life's staff, especially Richard Stolley, managing editor; John Loengard, picture editor; Steve Robinson, senior editor; Charles Whittingham, publisher; and Mary Davis, general manager. Instrumental help was also provided by Life Picture Service, and special thanks are given to Marthe Smith, manager. Thanks, too, are offered to photo researchers Peggy Kagan and Elaine Vogel.

FIRST EDITION

Designer: Barbara DuPree Knowles

Library of Congress Cataloging in Publication Data
Main entry under title:

LIFE in sports.

1. Sports—Pictorial works. I. Whittingham, Richard.
II. Life (Chicago, Ill.: 1978)   III. Life (Chicago, Ill.)
GV704.L54 1985   796'.022'2   85-42601
ISBN 0-06-015458-6

85 86 87 88 89 WAK 10 9 8 7 6 5 4 3 2 1

CONTENTS

FOREWORD

Life has always been a first-rate sports fan. Its photographers and writers have traveled the whole world to capture the pageant, action, and drama of athletic competition. From bullfights in Spain to the Olympic Games in Japan, crewing on the Thames to the World Series at Yankee Stadium, skiing the Swiss Alps to sailing the North Atlantic; at ringside, greenside, courtside, and trackside, *Life* photographers have recorded the manifold world of sport, preserving the historic moments, the memorable performances, and the inherent excitement that make it such a rich realm of entertainment.

When the first issue of *Life,* dated November 23, 1936, appeared, with the masthead listing of Henry Luce as managing editor and Daniel Longwell as picture editor, sport found its way into it. On one page was a photograph of the Emperor of Ethiopia, Haile Selassie, whiling away his exile by playing soccer in England. Later in the issue, a seven-picture essay, "Golfing Among the Gooney Birds," wove the pictorial story of how a Pan Am ground crew on Midway Island in the Pacific had laid out a nine-hole golf course and then discovered they had to share it with the swarms of albatrosses that also claimed the island as their home. Down the proverbial road awaited Kentucky Derbies, Olympic Games, championship boxing matches, Rose Bowls, Henley Regattas, Grand Prix auto races, and other assorted sports spectaculars.

While *Life* was still in its prenatal stage, its editors had thought that the photographic raw material for the magazine could be acquired almost in total from the news services. But as the reality of *Life* emerged, they soon found that would simply not work. To provide the visual effects for the broad-ranging stories planned for the picture magazine, the editors realized that those people taking the pictures must not only be masters of the art and techniques of photography but skilled journalists as well. The random action shots from news services served certain purposes, but much more was needed to flesh out the character of an illustrative story or provide the continuity to a photo essay.

So *Life* turned to its own photographers, a small but provocative list on the masthead of that first issue: Margaret Bourke-White, Alfred Eisenstaedt, Thomas D. McAvoy, and Peter Stackpole. It was in the second issue of *Life* that the first sports photograph taken by a staffer appeared, Peter Stackpole's portrait of a begrimed, dead-tired, 36-year-old New York Giant tackle by the name of Cal Hubbard, wondering perhaps, as he sat in the rain on the sideline at the Polo Grounds, if it was really all worth the $150 a game he earned in 1936 (page 191).

Since that time a procession of photographers unparalleled in their craft have left on the pages of *Life* a social history of the sporting world. George Silk provided his rapturous pictures of sailing and the intense excitement of competing for the America's Cup. Gjon Mili revolutionized action photography with his high-speed cameras and strobe lighting systems, freezing a pair of cocks in the frenzy of a fight or the thundering action in a polo match. Art Rickerby brought the sports photo essay to high art as his cameras seized the violence and velocity in sports like lacrosse, hockey, and World Cup soccer and blended the elements into exciting and informative pictorial stories.

There have been so many others too, all richly respected in the field of photography: Walter Iooss, Co Rentmeester, John Zimmerman, Hy Peskin, Rich Clarkson, Loomis Dean, Joe Scherschel, John Dominis, Wallace Kirkland, Larry Burrows, Myron Davis,

Michael Rougier, and Ralph Morse, to mention but a few represented on the ensuing pages of this book.

Life quickly inscribed a reputation of settling for only the best. Along with its photographers, the magazine sent Ernest Hemingway to cover the bullfights in Spain one year, Casey Stengel to provide his colorful observations of the World Series another time, and commissioned Norman Mailer to report on his beloved world of boxing. Ogden Nash brought his inimitable poetry to the pages of *Life,* lyricizing photo albums of those who played the games of football and baseball.

Above all, however, stand the pictures. "Most magazines are built around editors and writers," former managing editor Ralph Graves wrote in the Introduction to *The Best of Life,* "but *Life* was built around photographers. Their professional skill and unquenchable enterprise [are] at the heart of *Life's* success. . . . *Life* was first and always devoted to pictures."

In the elapsing years since 1936, *Life* was there to record Joe Louis pulverizing Max Schmeling, Tony Zale KO'ing Rocky Graziano and Rocky Graziano KO'ing Tony Zale, Bill Veeck's midget when he came to bat for the St. Louis Browns, and Bobby Thomson's historic home run at the Polo Grounds "heard round the world." *Life* was at the finish line when Roger Bannister broke the 4-minute mile, on the sideline as Frank Gifford raced around end for a Southern Cal touchdown, in the stadiums where Bob Mathias won the Olympic decathlon and Mary Decker took her famous Olympic fall, even with Grantland Rice as he talked sports over lunch at Toots Shor's.

Life has captured the legends in action: Ali, Manolete, DiMaggio and Williams, Blanchard and Davis, Hogan and Snead, Kramer and Gonzales, Didrickson-Zaharias, Citation, Landy and Bannister, Sonja Henie, Hull and Orr, Arcaro, Chamberlain and Russell, Spitz, Korbut—the list glitters on and on.

Life has also observed Hemingway as he fished the Caribbean, Bing Crosby boxing, Woody Allen playing billiards, Ronald Reagan at equestrian pursuits, and Hubert

Humphrey donkey-fighting. The magazine's photographers have gone on an imperial duck hunt in Japan, to a marbles match in Michigan, a polar bear club swim in Moscow, cormorant fishing in China, the roller derby, a six-day bike race, and to snap a baseball player who pitched while standing on his head.

Just as it has on the newsfronts of the world, at the movies, in the arts, and among the folkways of our time, *Life* in sports has lived up to Henry Luce's grand plan for the magazine, which he eloquently described before publication of the first issue in 1936: "To see life; to see the world; to eyewitness great events; to watch the faces of the poor and the gestures of the proud; to see strange things . . . to see and take pleasure in seeing; to see and be amazed; to see and be instructed."

—Richard Whittingham

IN SPORTS

1/CONFRONTATIONS

The year was 1959 and in Spain it was billed as the most spectacular sporting event of the century: a series of bullfights matching a brave old champion of the ring and a brilliant young challenger.

The rival matadors were Luis Miguel Dominguín, then 33, and Antonio Ordóñez, 27, brother-in-law of Dominguín and his good friend. Dominguín was considered by most Spaniards to be *numero uno,* the first in the bullring. Twelve years earlier, coincidentally, Manolete was the *numero uno* of the time, and in his effort to remain that he was forced into taking chances he ought not to have taken and was fatally gored. The young challenger who forced him to take those chances was Luis Miguel Dominguín.

Now it was Dominguín's turn to step down. At the meetings with Ordóñez, called *mano a mano* (hand to hand), each matador took on three bulls and was rewarded with the trophies of ears, hooves, or tails. Both matadors put on grand exhibitions. But Dominguín lagged behind his young rival in the judgment of most critics and was pushed into recklessness. Gored several times as the *mano a mano* moved from city to city, he lost his *numero uno* ranking to Ordóñez. Unlike Manolete, he survived with a few scars to remind him of the confrontations.

▶ A triumphant entrance into the bullring at Bayonne. Ordóñez (*left*) and Dominguín (*right*) lead the elaborate and traditional procession at the start of the day's six-fight program. Behind them are each matador's retinue of picadors, banderilleros, and sword handlers.

A casual Dominguín displays an attitude of unconcern as he performs a difficult high pass, leading the angry bull perilously close to his hip.

▶ A display of courage and confidence by Ordóñez, kneeling dangerously close to the bull's horns. The bull has been momentarily mesmerized into inaction after a series of passes. The display by Ordóñez is a brief one, however, because the bull will quickly recover and resume the fight. ▼ Ordóñez smoothly completes a low pass with his *muleta*, a small red cape, as he leads the bull around him during *faena,* the last act of the fight before the kill.

Dominguín, attempting an especially daring pass, fails and is tossed by the enraged bull. His assistants, however, were able to divert the bull a moment later to prevent a further goring. Dominguín, bloodied and soiled, rose and returned to kill the bull.

The moment of truth. Ordóñez carefully sights along his sword, preparing to make the fatal thrust. Moments later the bull lay dead and Antonio Ordóñez was *numero uno.*

German hopeful Max Schmeling came to America to fetch the world heavyweight crown. He found Joe Louis unwilling to give it up. Here in their 1938 fight, almost unconscious, he hangs on the rope before going down for the final count.

Among the most classic and enduring confrontations, man and the mountain. English climbers edge precariously along an ice-covered Swiss alp in this spectacular photograph taken in 1938.

In the history of boxing, there were no more brutal and hard-fought contests than those waged by Tony Zale and Rocky Graziano. Somebody up there apparently didn't like Graziano in the photo at the right, shown as he goes down for the count after middleweight champion Zale connected with a thunderous left hook in this 1946 title bout. Less than a year later it was Graziano's turn— a murderous right sends Zale reeling just a few moments before Graziano put him away and took the world middleweight crown.

The inevitable hockey sideshow, this one staged by Bobby Orr (*on top*) of the Boston Bruins and Pat Quinn of the Toronto Maple Leafs. Orr, at age 21 in this 1970 photo and just starting on his way to becoming a legend in the sport, had in hockey already earned three knee operations, a broken collarbone, a dislocated shoulder, two broken noses, and cuts requiring fifty stitches.

► Confrontations in karate can be painful. When this picture was taken in 1947, few people in America had ever heard of a sport called karate. But *Life* brought it to the nation's attention. Karate came to the United States from Japan after World War II, although paradoxically it had been outlawed in Japan during the war because it was considered "foreign." ▼ The two Joe Louis–Billy Conn fights of the 1940s were among the best of that decade. In this 1941 bout, their first meeting, Louis, the reigning champ, found out just how good a boxer Conn was. Jabs and combinations like this from the lightning-fast Conn kept Louis on the brink of defeat through almost 13 rounds. But just before the bell, the Brown Bomber found his mark and KO'd the young contender.

A most uncommon sight, Joe Louis on the canvas, the result of a flurry of punches from Jersey Joe Walcott, his onetime sparring partner, in this 1947 heavyweight title fight. The 33-year-old Louis went down again but managed to get back up and last the 15 rounds. Walcott, a decided underdog who one writer before the fight suggested would do well to sell advertising space on his shoe soles, appeared to most to be the winner. But the decision went to the champ, Louis. Walcott would lose to Louis again the following year but eventually gain the heavyweight title in 1951 by knocking out Ezzard Charles.

23

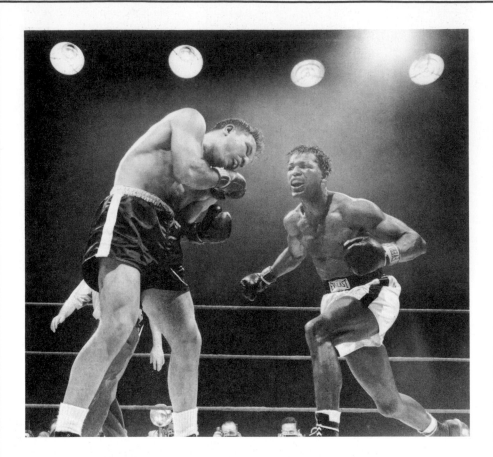

The raging bull, Jake LaMotta, is about to take one on the chin from Sugar Ray Robinson. LaMotta, the middleweight champion, had fought Robinson five times previously and lost four of them. He lost this one and the title a few moments after this picture was taken when the referee stopped the fight in the thirteenth round.

They called him the "beatnik of the bullring" because of the length of his hair, long by 1965 standards, and spectators hurled loaves of bread at him when they felt his performance was subpar, but El Cordobés was the rage of the bullfighting world in those days. Unorthodox in style—he would often taunt or sneer at the bull, slap it with his sword, even punch it in the nose—his cape work was masterful as he clearly illustrates in this fight in the ring at Nimes.

Friendly in confrontation, Rafer Johnson of the United States (*right*) and Russia's Vasily Kuznetsov greet each other during a 1958 track meet in Moscow where both superathletes competed in the decathlon. The 22-year-old Johnson, who was also UCLA's student body president, won by compiling 8302 points, at that time the most ever scored in the event. Johnson broke that record 2 years later by scoring 8392 to win the decathlon in the 1960 Olympic Games.

This was the kind of night it was all night long for Ezzard Charles in Yankee Stadium as the onetime heavyweight champ tried to regain his title from enthroned Rocky Marciano. Charles endured 15 rounds in this 1954 fight, but Marciano won it by unanimous decision. It was Marciano's forty-sixth victory in as many professional fights, forty of which had been won by knockouts.

◄ The unique angle of this photo catches college-grad challenger Chuck Davey on the way to one of his four trips to the canvas as welterweight champ Kid Gavilan raises his fists in triumph. Davey was unable to come out for the tenth round of this 1953 fight. ▼ Rocky Marciano's victim here is a dazed Archie Moore, holder of the light heavyweight title and aspirant to the heavyweight crown. Moore went down for the count in the ninth round of this 1955 fight. It was Marciano's last title fight; he retired undefeated the following year.

▲ A 36-year-old Sugar Ray Robinson still has what it takes as he sends Bobo Olson, 9 years his junior, to what one writer termed "palookaville." It was the fourth consecutive time Robinson whipped Olson. Olson had held the middleweight title from 1953 to 1955 after Sugar Ray had abandoned it, but he lost it when Robinson decided to return to the ring. ▶ Sugar Ray Robinson was 38 years old in 1958 when he got in the ring with Carmen Basilio to try to regain the middleweight title he had lost to Basilio the year before. The little bit of thunder from Robinson's right was one of the contributing factors to Sugar Ray's successful recapture of the crown.

It was this punch, stunning Sonny Liston, and a few others like it that propelled 22-year-old Cassius Clay in 1964 into the elite class known as heavyweight champions of the world, the second youngest in the history of the sport. He dethroned Liston in 6 lopsided rounds. Liston tried a comeback a year later but Clay finished his career with a first-round knockout.

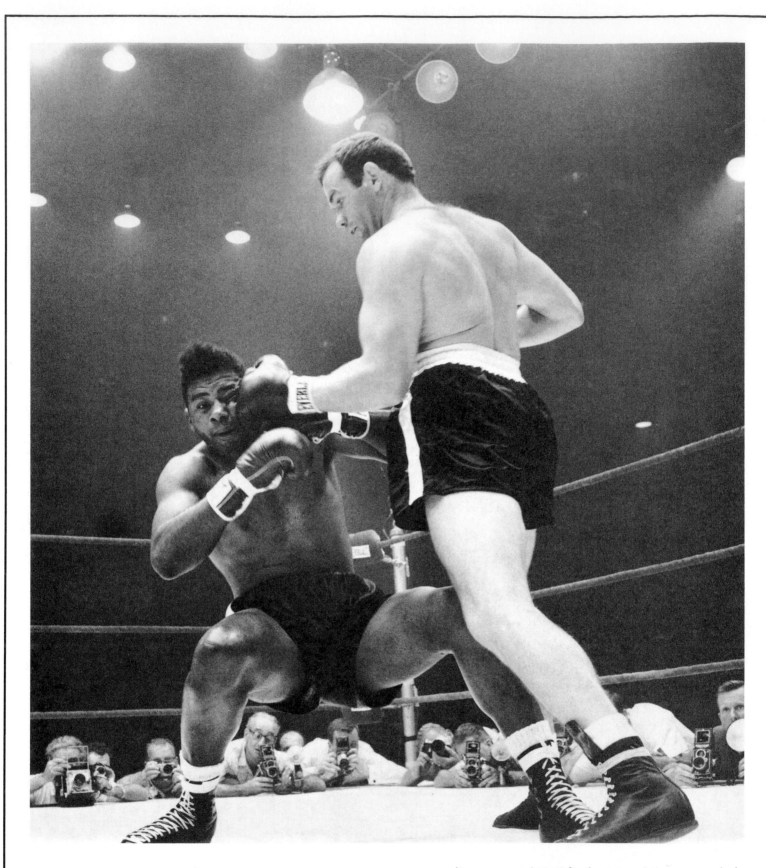

It was a good start for Ingemar Johansson, challenger from Sweden, when in the first round of their 1961 title fight he landed a right and then a quick left to batter heavyweight champion Floyd Patterson to the canvas. Johansson decked Patterson twice that round but the champ got up and floored Johansson before the 3 minutes elapsed. Patterson caught Johansson again in the sixth round and that ended the fight, leaving Patterson the champ.

Muhammad Ali showed up at Joe Frazier's training camp for a little promotional face-off before their upcoming heavyweight title fight in 1971. It was only a matter of words when the two hammed it up for the camera. A few weeks later, however, words would turn to punches and, after a full and brutal 15 rounds, Smokin' Joe Frazier won by decision.

2/BASEBALL

► Satchel Paige was a cool customer on and off the field, pictured in both places here in 1941: before a Black Yankees game at Yankee Stadium and on the fender of his car on a street in Harlem. One of the game's truly great pitchers, Paige began hurling professionally sometime in the 1920s and spent most of his long career in the Negro leagues and barnstorming with Negro teams in the United States, the Caribbean, and Central America. At age 42 in 1948, after baseball became integrated, he made it to the majors and spent two years with the Cleveland Indians and three with the St. Louis Browns. At age 59 he came back and pitched three scoreless innings for the Kansas City Athletics.

◄ In the house that he built, Yankee Stadium, an ailing Babe Ruth bends to the microphone that will carry his voice beyond his former ballpark to every other stadium where games were to be played that afternoon of April 27, 1947. With a voice hoarse and broken, the 52-year-old Ruth thanked his legion of fans throughout the country for the tributes paid to him that day. It was a grand and plaintive farewell, and a little more than a year later the Babe was dead of cancer.

To hype the 1947 baseball season in Pittsburgh, a bowlegged Honus Wagner struck this pose to frame the Pirate batboy. The Flying Dutchman, as he was known, played shortstop for Pittsburgh from 1900 through 1917 and became one of the game's certified legends. But there wasn't much he could do for the cellar-destined Pirates of 1947.

When Fiorello LaGuardia, the "Little Flower" and one of New York's most colorful mayors, threw out the first ball, he did it with style. This opening toss launched the 1936 baseball season.

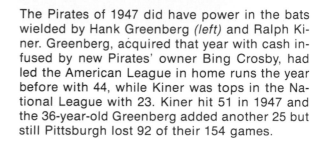

The Pirates of 1947 did have power in the bats wielded by Hank Greenberg *(left)* and Ralph Kiner. Greenberg, acquired that year with cash infused by new Pirates' owner Bing Crosby, had led the American League in home runs the year before with 44, while Kiner was tops in the National League with 23. Kiner hit 51 in 1947 and the 36-year-old Greenberg added another 25 but still Pittsburgh lost 92 of their 154 games.

The classic swing. All the rhythm and power are evident as Joe DiMaggio lashes out a double in the 1949 All-Star game. The Yankee Clipper was earning $100,000 that year and was just coming off a heel injury that had kept him out of the lineup for most of the first half of the season. The catcher, in this first All-Star game in which blacks played, is Roy Campanella.

Another classic swing. Ted Williams drives one out of the park in spring training before the 1948 season. "The Splendid Splinter," as he was known in those days, followed up with—for him—a little better than average year, batting .369, but a bit short of his career best of .406 six years earlier.

Ewell "The Whip" Blackwell and his famous sidearm delivery are caught in this two-stage stroboscopic photo in 1947. It was the best year in Blackwell's ten-season career, 22 wins against only 8 defeats.

The fastest arm in town, Bob Feller, is about to unleash his legendary fastball here in 1951. A strikeout king and perennial 20-game winner, Feller was instrumental in the success of the Cleveland Indians in the 1940s and early 1950s.

Portrait of a rookie, who, as *Life* suggested in 1948, "might have stepped right out of the pages of Ring Lardner into the training camp of the Boston Red Sox." The spindly, smiling southpaw from Elizabeth, New Jersey, was Mickey McDermott, who managed to stick with the Red Sox that year and stay around the major leagues for twelve seasons.

▲ Famed for the chaw of tobacco in his cheek, Nellie Fox of the Chicago White Sox throws over the slide of Ted Williams to complete a double play in this 1951 game. The White Sox shortstop is Chico Carrasquel. ▼ Bobby Thomson is swarmed on by jubilant New York Giant teammates at home plate after hitting his famous three-run homer to win the National League playoffs in 1951. Losing to the Brooklyn Dodgers 4–2 in the bottom of the ninth, Thomson took a strike from reliever Ralph Branca, then pasted the next pitch into the left-field seats at the Polo Grounds, a home run that became known as "the shot heard round the world."

Eddie Gaedel, at 3 feet 7 inches, the shortest player in baseball history, takes one high in this immortal photo from the 1951 season. Admittedly inspired by a story by James Thurber that appeared in *The Saturday Evening Post* some 10 years previous, St. Louis Browns' owner Bill Veeck secretly signed midget Gaedel to a contract and sent him up to bat for the Browns before an almost full house in St. Louis in a game against the Detroit Tigers. Detroit pitcher Bob Cain walked him on four pitches. When questioned after the game as to why he allowed it, umpire Ed Hurley said, "The midget's contract was in order. We go by that, not by a tape measure." Nevertheless, two days later American League officials recommended a new rule: no more midgets.

In 1952 Bill Veeck brought in a true baseball titan to manage his St. Louis Browns, Rogers Hornsby. The Rajah, who had been out of baseball since 1937, was given the mission of getting the Browns out of last place, but he stayed around for only about a third of the season before moving to the National League and the Cincinnati Reds.

◀ The chief reason the St. Louis Cardinals were so good during the 1940s and 1950s, Stan ''The Man'' Musial chats here with his manager in 1952 Eddie Stanky. Seven times Musial took the National League batting crown, and over his 22 years with the Cardinals had a lifetime average of .331.

◀ A determined President Dwight D. Eisenhower, once a semipro outfielder himself, lets fly the first ball to launch the Washington Senators' 1953 season. At the left and behind Ike is Michigan Senator Homer Ferguson, directly behind is Speaker of the House Joe Martin of Massachusetts, and to the right of the President are Vice President Richard Nixon and Washington Senator owner Clark Griffith.

▶ A scene that haunted many a batter, Whitey Ford delivers a fastball strike in this 1953 game. The 24-year-old Yankee southpaw had just come back from 2 years in the army, drafted after his rookie year in 1950. In the article that accompanied this picture, Life suggested that the Yankees, who had just won four consecutive American League pennants, might just win four more on the strength of the youthful Ford's arm. (They didn't win four straight, but they did win four out of the next five.)

◄ Ogden Nash wrote the caption for this photo in a special *Life* essay in 1955 describing some of the greats of the day in his own inimitable way:

This holler guy who we are follering,
What does he holler when he's hollering?
You can hear him clean to hell and gone,
C'mon there baby, c'mon, c'mon!
Or he will change his holler, maybe,
To let's go, baby, baby, baby!
He uses a plug of tobacco per game,
And has never lost or swallowed same.
Nellie Fox so lives to play
That every day's a hollerday.

▶ A dance to baseball? Actually it's Willie Mays *(left)* and Whitey Lockman going after a pop-up at the New York Giants 1954 spring training camp in Phoenix, Arizona.

An uncommon sight as Roy Campanella, the Brooklyn Dodgers' great catcher, throws wildly over the glove of Billy Cox in a 1954 game against the New York Giants at the Polo Grounds. The two teams were embroiled in a hot pennant race, which the Giants eventually won.

Big Don Newcombe, about to blaze a fastball here, was the keystone of the Dodgers' pitching staff in 1955, winning 20 games and losing only 5. "Newk," as the other Boys of Summer called him, was essential in getting Brooklyn to the World Series that year. The batter here is Ransom Jackson of the Chicago Cubs.

Elston Howard of the New York Yankees lunges for a high throw in this 1955 game, but Detroit Tiger pitcher Billy Hoeft scores anyway.

In a darkened Ebbets Field, 33,000 Dodger fans hold lighted matches as part of a tribute to team captain Pee Wee Reese in 1955. It was the thirty-sixth birthday of the man they called the "Little Colonel," who had been slotted at shortstop since 1940 with the exception of a few years during World War II.

◄ Ted Williams, one of baseball's quintessential hitters was always generous with instruction on the finer points of the art. Here in the Red Sox clubhouse he passes on a tip or two to rookie Gordon Windhorn in 1956.

▶ Caught wet-handed is Milwaukee Braves' pitcher Lew Burdette, who was accused several times of throwing spitballs during the 1956 season.

This unique multiple-exposure picture of a Mickey Mantle home run, taken by *Life* staffer Ralph Morse at Cleveland's Municipal Stadium in 1956, shows Mantle hitting the ball, rounding first base, second, third, and then being congratulated by teammate Joe Collins. The pitcher, catcher, and third baseman are shown at the moment Mantle hit the ball; the first and second baseman at the time he jogs around the bases.

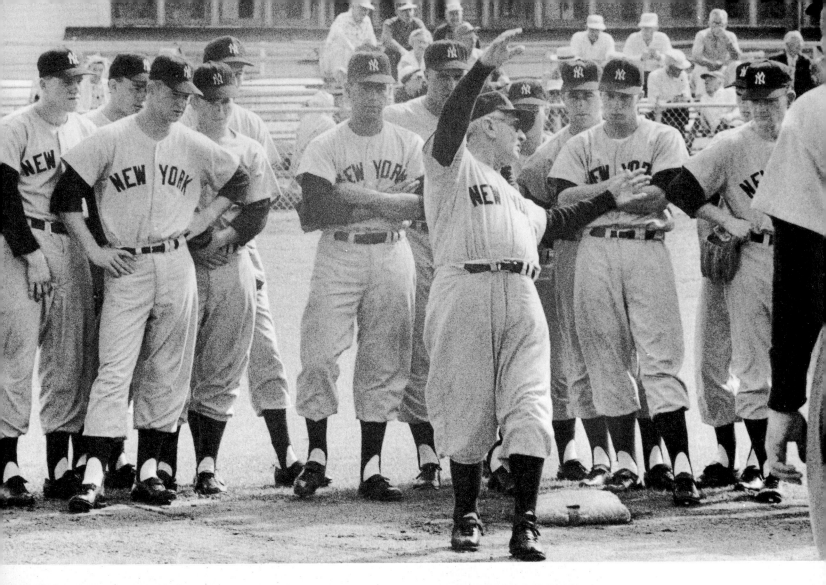

The "Old Perfesser," Casey Stengel, is not teaching a dance step to his class of rookies at spring training in St. Petersburg, Florida, in this 1957 photo. Actually he's demonstrating what to watch for in a pitcher's foot movements.

About to do what he did 755 times in the major leagues, Hank Aaron is set to stroke a home run. At this point in his career, 1957, he still had about 675 to go to become the all-time home run king.

The hangdog looks of Yogi Berra and Mickey Mantle say it all. The mighty New York Yankees on this day in 1959 have fallen into the American League cellar. No Yankee team in the preceding 19 years had sunk to last place at any time during a season. The year before they had won the World Series, and they would rise from the cellar to third place before the 1959 season ended.

The past recaptured. Birdie Tebbetts, onetime top-notch catcher for the Detroit Tigers and Boston Red Sox, dons the mitt once again to give some tips to a young minor league hopeful.

Billy Martin is announcing that his team, the Minnesota Twins, are in first place. The Twins stayed at the top of the American League West in 1969, which was also Martin's rookie year as a manager.

The hazards of a photographer are varied. *Life* staffer Michael Mauney snapped Cubs manager Leo Durocher's casually flipped bat in mid-air, then ducked out of the way before being beaned by it.

◀ Johnny Bench was only 22 years old when he lashed out this double for the Cincinnati Reds in 1970, but he was already being talked about in the same league of catchers as Mickey Cochrane, Bill Dickey, Roy Campanella, and Yogi Berra.

▼ Back to visit his old ballclub for the first time after being paralyzed in an automobile accident, Roy Campanella chats with a young fan at Dodgertown in Vero Beach, Florida, at spring training 1959. Looking on is Dodger owner Walter O'Malley, who had just hired the former Brooklyn Dodger catcher to work in the front office of what was now the Los Angeles Dodgers.

Framed by the legs of a Chicago White Sox coach, Luis Aparicio dives back to first in a crucial game with the Cleveland Indians late in the 1959 season. Late with the tag is Indian first baseman Vic Power. A few days later, the "Go-Go Sox," as they were called because of their hustle and prowess on the base paths, took the American League pennant, their first since the infamous, game-throwing Black Sox of 1919.

Roger Maris, headed for the outfield after his last time at bat in game 154 of the 1961 season. With 59 home runs, he had hoped to break Babe Ruth's record in the same number of games. During the next eight games, however, he would hit numbers 60 and 61 to set the single-season standard.

Mickey Mantle, his knees painfully giving out on him in 1965 after 14 years in the big leagues, evinces the anguish of knowing that his career on the field is moving all too quickly to its inevitable end.

Surfing in Australia goes beyond sport and into the realm of high adventure. On this day of 15-foot waves in 1958 near Sydney, ex-surfboard champion Serge Denman rides the slope of a comber chased by the swirling surf as his less adept companion heads into the water. If such titanic waves were not action enough, there are also vicious cross rip tides and treacherous undertows, not to mention the sharks which almost continually cruise just beyond the line of breakers and not infrequently claim an errant surfer or swimmer.

▲ An exuberant Alice Marble leaps the net in triumph back in 1939 and is frozen in the act by Gjon Mili's high-speed camera. One of the first great American women tennis players, Marble won the U.S. singles championship that year, as she had the year before and as she would the following year. ▶ A youthful Bobby Riggs in action was also captured by Gjon Mili in 1938. The photo was made at a speed of 1/100,000 of a second with the aid of a high-speed lighting system developed by Mili and a colleague. The next year Riggs took the singles title both in the United States and at Wimbledon.

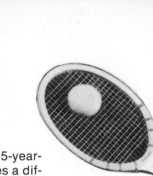

◄ With pigtails flying, 15-year-old Andrea Mead executes a difficult jump-turn on the slopes at Sun Valley, Idaho, as she prepares for the 1948 winter Olympics. But she would have to wait until 1952 for her gold medals, which she captured in Oslo, Norway, for both the women's slalom and the giant slalom.

► Sonja Henie was the first of the world-renowned figure skaters, and by 1936 she had won three Olympic gold medals, her first at age 16, and ten world championships. The tiny Norwegian later parlayed her figure skating skills and her supreme sense of showmanship into a career in motion pictures and as the star of her own extravagant touring ice revues.

Tennis greats Pancho Gonzales *(top)* and Jack Kramer were the most exciting racket wielders in America in the late 1940s, and their fierce competition brought the sport unprecedented publicity. Kramer won the U.S. singles championship in 1946 and 1947, and Gonzales took that title the next 2 years.

Ben Hogan is caught precisely as he makes contact, the concentration of the man and the tension of the moment sculpted in his face. When this picture was taken in 1955, Hogan was already a golfing legend: winner of four U.S. Opens, two Masters Tournaments, the PGA, and the British Open.

▼ Babe Didrickson-Zaharias saw action on a variety of sporting fields and was admired as one of the great women athletes of all time. She went to the Olympic Games in Los Angeles in 1932 and took gold medals in the javelin throw and the 80-meter hurdles, prompting Grantland Rice to write, "You are looking at the most flawless section of muscle harmony, of complete mental and physical coordination the world of sport has ever seen." She went on to barnstorm the United States, dipping her talented hands in baseball (she pitched in major league exhibition games), touring with her own basketball team, and, of course, leaving an indelible mark on women's golf, winning the U.S. Open three times. Here she drives from a tee at the All-American Golf Tournament in Chicago in 1953, having just recovered from a cancer operation. The next year she won the Open, but two years later she succumbed to cancer at the age of 42.

▲ The Reverend Bob Richards soars 14 feet, 9¼ inches to win the pole vault event at a meet in Mexico in 1955, an impressive height in the days before the fiberglass pole. Richards, the best vaulter of his time, won gold medals in the event in the 1952 and 1956 Olympics.

▶ The combination of grace, strength, and fluid motion embodied in the discus thrower inspired sculptors in ancient Greece. Here it is embodied in Fortune Gordien as he whirls to unleash the classic platter while trying to qualify for the team that would represent the United States in the 1948 Olympics in London.

▼ In 1947 Barbara Ann Scott was described as "a shy, blue-eyed, 18-year-old Canadian beauty, who is also the finest woman figure skater in the world." She lived up to the billing the following year at St. Moritz, Switzerland, where she won the Olympic gold medal.

▶ One of Europe's most lustrous ski events around the mid-twentieth century was the Arlberg-Kandahar races, set in the awesome Swiss Alps at Murren. Surrounded by jagged peaks (the famous Eiger at the left and part of the Jungfrau to the right), a slalom racer winds his way past picturesque chateaus in this 1950 competition. It was here at the Arlberg-Kandahar in 1928 that slalom and downhill racing were first introduced, and shortly thereafter both were recognized by the International Ski Federation.

This stunning portrait in silhouette of a platform diver was captured on film by *Life's* John Dominis in 1956.

A world's record in the making. Valeri Brumel of the Soviet Union barely clears the bar at 7 feet, 5 inches in 1962. The bar quivered as Brumel hurtled to the sawdust, a moment after this shot was taken, but it did not fall.

Althea Gibson was the first great black tennis player. At 5 feet, 10½ inches, she combined reach with power to win both the women's singles championship of the U.S. Open Tennis Tournament and the title at Wimbledon in 1957 and 1958. Here at the French championship in 1956 she exhibits the stride that enabled her to cover the court with consummate ease.

It is a rare sport indeed that provides more sustained action than hockey. Fast, physical, often violent, it is a game of flashing steel skates, menacingly wielded sticks, and hard-rubber pucks that can scream through the air at speeds in excess of 100 miles per hour. Hockey players carry more scars and probably less teeth than those who battle in any other organized sport.

The sport's following is dedicated, often fanatic, and its fans can be as animated in the stands as the players are on the ice. In this essay for *Life* in 1968, staff photographer Arthur Rickerby dramatically captures the excitement, fierce competition, and mayhem they come out to watch.

► When the puck is in front of the goal, it is a meeting of savage consequence. Or, as *Life* described this particular meeting: "The scramble at the goal mouth is a maelstrom—and the supreme moment of lance-to-lance combat." No. 9 is Bobby Hull of the Chicago Black Hawks, one of the game's all-time greats because of his dazzling speed on the ice and what was considered the most wicked slapshot in the sport.

▼ A Boston Bruin delivers a body check here to send Toronto's Alan Stanley smashing into the rink's protective glass shield as a teammate *(right)* streaks toward the Maple Leaf goal.

Careening out of control here is Bob Rousseau of the Montreal Canadians, who will feel the results of it in the morning. Spills at high speed are a consistent crowd pleaser.

69

But nothing brings the fans to their feet quicker
than when opposing players become unhappy
with each other and show their displeasure in
the same manner that Ted Harris (10) of the Montreal Canadians does here.

The competition was intense for the figure skating crown of 1956 when these two young American girls hit the ice. ◀ Tenley Albright, a junior at Radcliffe College, had won the world figure skating championship the year before. ▲ Runner-up was 15-year-old Carol Heiss. The more experienced Tenley took the Olympic gold that year, but Carol captured the world championship crown, which she then proceeded to monopolize each year through 1960, the same year she won the gold at the Olympic Games.

A youthful Manolete demonstrates his brave and graceful technique by executing a difficult, back-to-the-bull pass in Mexico City in 1946. Called by his fans *El Monstro* (The Monster), Manolete was at the acme of his career and attracted almost hysterical adulation, but a little more than a year later he would be gored to death in the ring at Linares, Spain.

To catch this remarkable photo of hammer thrower Ed Bagdonas, *Life's* George Silk used a version of a photo-finish camera with no shutter. The film is drawn past a narrow aperture, snapping Bagdonas as he moves into and across the camera's narrow field of vision.

Billie Jean King was 23 years old when she smashed this ball over the net back in 1967, the year she won the singles, doubles, and mixed doubles titles in both the United States and Britain. During her career in the 1960s and 1970s she won an unprecedented twenty Wimbledon titles in singles and doubles as well as four U.S. singles crowns. She was, of course, one of the key figures in establishing women's professional tennis and rooting it firmly in the American consciousness when she defeated Bobby Riggs in 1973 before a television audience estimated at more than 50 million.

▲ Driving a towering wall of water into the air, water ski champion Chuck Stearns is taking a celebration, slalom-style ride after having just broken the world speed record in his sport in 1967. Riding on a single ski he sped up an estuary in Long Beach, California, at 119.52 miles per hour. ▼ Hockey great Bobby Orr shows a bit of grim determination in front of the goal in this 1970 game. The Boston Bruins thought so highly of his potential that they signed Orr to a contract when he was only 14 years old. At 18, he was the NHL's rookie of the year, and after that it was merely superstar status as he led the Bruins to two Stanley Cup titles.

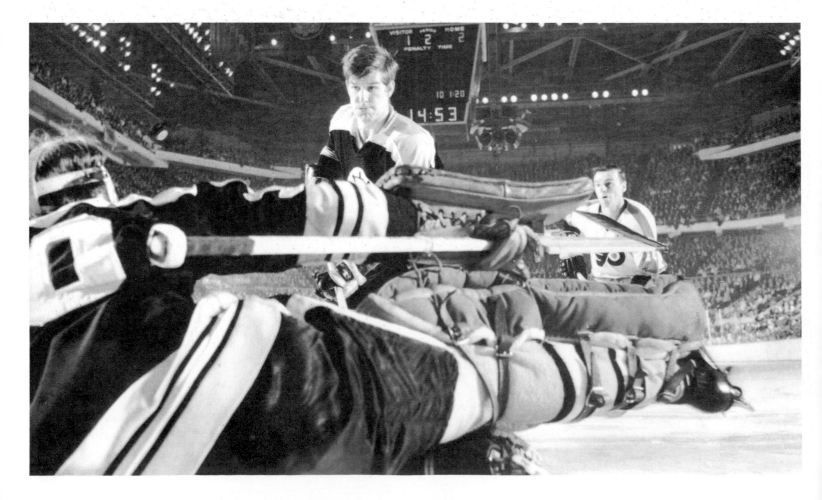

"Riding the Wild Waves" is the way *Life* entitled this 1963 photo essay, describing the action in the waters off Hawaii this way:

When waves kindled by some faraway storm reach the awesome height of 30 feet off Oahu's northern beaches most men gasp and stare. But a very small, courageous band of surfers, mostly expatriates from California and Australia, get on their boards and risk their lives on the mountainous crests of foaming fury in a sport every bit as exhilarating—and nearly as dangerous—as skiing over Niagara on a barrel stave.

The men who ride the big ones in Hawaii actually ski down the shoulder of a wave away from the curl. They call the first breathtaking schuss "taking the drop." Their boards rapidly accelerate up to 35 miles an hour and kick up waves like speedboats. And a merciless mauling awaits the unfortunate who doesn't complete his ride. He is driven downward by the appalling maelstrom, tossed around, sucked back down and, frequently, after fighting up for a desperate gulp of air, hammered down again by the next wave.

The thrill and peril of it are recorded here by *Life's* own George Silk.

▼ A unique view of a big-wave surfer in action. Nick Beck of Honolulu assumes a balanced crouch at the top of a wave as his board moves through the water at about 20 miles per hour. At the precise moment he took the picture here (by activating a camera on the front of his board with a string wrapped around his left hand) Beck was at the most apprehensive moment of the ride, hovering just before he would plunge down the face of the wave and race diagonally away from its looming crest.

Running before the savage sea, a surfer at Oahu's Sunset Beach deftly executes a right-hand slide under a thundering 15-footer.

This surfer tries a free-fall down a 22-foot wave only to be flipped like a coin. The real peril here, however, is the surfboard slicing through the water at high speed. Being hit by a rampaging surfboard is the most common cause of injury or death in big-wave surfing.

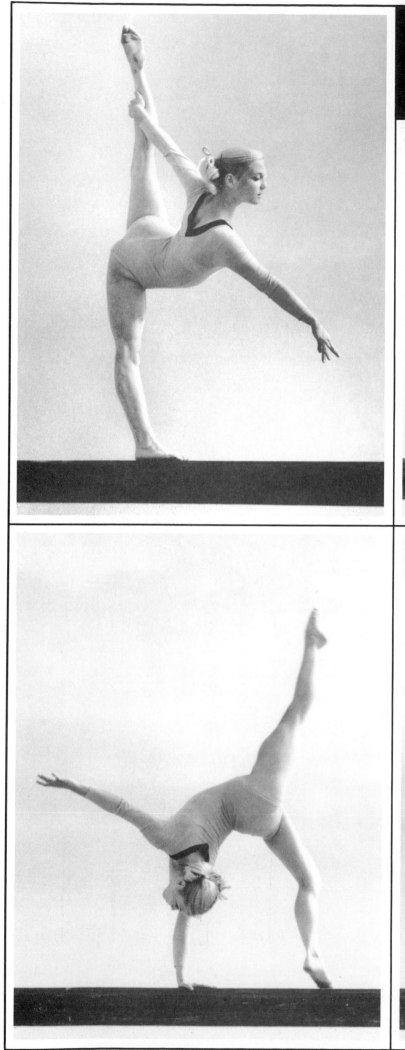

A classic ballet on the balance beam is performed by Cathy Rigby in this 1972 sequence. The diminutive 19-year-old, who stood just under 5 feet tall and weighed a mere 90 pounds, performed with fearless precision on the 4-inch wide plank and emerged as America's premier female gymnast.

In 1968, they used terms like "rocketing," "lightninglike," "thunderous" to describe Arthur Ashe's serve. Coordination, timing, and whiplike drive were what made it so effective. And he used it to take titles in both the United States and Britain.

One of sportsdom's most unique couples, photographed in 1972, Hal and Olga Connolly of the United States and Czechoslovakia, respectively, he throwing the hammer and she heaving a 16-pound shot (a training exercise). Both had been competing in the Olympics since the 1956 get-together in Melbourne, Australia, where he won a gold medal in the hammer throw and she a bronze in the discus. Four months after they met in 1956 they ignored the cold war and were married in Prague. Both made trips to the Olympics in Rome, Tokyo, and Mexico City over the next 12 years and, when these pictures were taken, Hal at 40 and Olga at 39 were in the process of honing their skills and beefing their strength for the 1972 games at Munich.

▲ *Life* covered a new sport in 1971, body surfing, which was developed along a shore at Newport Beach, California, where board surfing was impossible because the waves broke so steeply and unexpectedly. A few brave and reckless souls devised a technique that used nothing but the body to ride the huge waves and to suffer the batterings of roiling surf and impacted sand. The body surfer here is on his way to a most bruising encounter with the shore. Catapulted in at full speed he is about to be dashed into water that is only 6 inches deep.

▶ Peggy Fleming was a 19-year-old student at Colorado College when she executed this elegant lay-back spin in 1968. Four years earlier she won her first national championship and the then 15-year-old came in sixth in the Olympic competition at Innsbruck, Austria. At 5 feet, 3 inches tall, 109 pounds, and with an appearance of chinalike fragility, she was dubbed the "Bambi of the Blades." A five-time U.S. champion and with three world titles behind her when this picture was taken, she had little difficulty capturing the gold medal at the 1968 winter Olympics at Grenoble, France.

4/CELEBRITIES AT SPORT

▶ Ernest Hemingway, devoted deep-sea fisherman, with his catch of marlin, Key West, Florida, 1938. *Life* followed Hemingway's sporting life from fishing off Florida and Cuba and in the trout streams of Idaho to big-game hunting in Africa and to the bullrings of Spain.

Ronald Reagan was still officially a movie actor when this photo appeared in *Life* in early 1966. But the adroit horse jumper, aboard Nancy D here, launched his political career by becoming California's governor before the year was out.

Crooner Bing Crosby had a mean left hook, it was said, but not too many people knew about it. Here Crosby *(right)* spars with ex-middleweight champ Freddie Steele, whom he managed, in 1938.

President Dwight D. Eisenhower, a dedicated golfer, works on his approach shot on the south lawn of the White House in 1953. To get a little exercise when he wasn't worrying about the Korean War or the ever colder war with Russia, Ike had this stretch of the White House grounds fashioned into a driving fairway. His valet served as caddy and ball fetcher.

▲ It is not the House of David baseball team; it is Fidel Castro *(uniformed player to the left)* who pitched in a baseball game in Havana in 1959 shortly after he and his forces took control of the country. His bearded batterymate is Cuban army chief Cienfuegos.

◄ The impeccably dressed hunter in tweed suit, hat, and soft leather gloves and braced by a portable stool is Generalissimo Francisco Franco on a duck hunt in the spring of 1949 in Arunjuez, Spain, about 30 miles from Madrid. *Life* described him that year as "an affable country squire and sportsman . . . [who] has executed and tortured a great many people, but he has never been a strutting jut-jawed dictator in the Mussolini mold. He finds the Spartan life distasteful and long ago learned that he could kill just as many ducks at noon as in the cold and bitter dawn." On this noontime sortie, Franco and his party bagged about 40 ducks.

Hubert Humphrey is caught here engaging in one of the world's more esoteric sports, donkey fighting. The amateur matador, waving a *muleta* of canvas before a frisky Abyssinian jackass named Pietro, was Vice President in 1965 when this photo was taken.

◄ Proud fisherman Harry S. Truman displays a king salmon. The President later admitted it was not he who caught the fish. Truman had one sport, however, that he practiced regularly: bowling (he had an alley built in the White House).

▲ He was in fact a real senator who toiled in the Capitol building, but Eugene McCarthy suited up for the 1968 baseball battle between congressional Democrats and Republicans. Earlier in the year he'd lost out in a bid for the Democratic presidential nomination, but earlier in life he was a highly regarded first baseman on a semipro team in his home state of Minnesota.

◄ Taking a little time off from commanding the American forces in Vietnam is General William Westmoreland in 1966. The general played tennis regularly at the *Cercle Sportif* in Saigon in those days, and he was described as a player with "little style but enormous energy [who] likes to whack the daylights out of the ball and if he feels his opponent isn't making him run enough [roars] 'Hey, you're letting up on me!' "

◄ Then Vice President Spiro Agnew was a terror on the tennis courts in 1970, as famous for driving tennis balls into the backs of his partners as another, later vice president, Gerald Ford, was for driving golf balls into crowds of spectators.

▼ The exuberant golfer is Rose Kennedy, a long-time devotee of the game, toning up her iron shots here on the lawn of the Kennedy compound at Hyannis Port.

Woody Allen, who *Life* in 1967 called a "shy extrovert," often sought solitude in those days in a concentrated game of billiards.

Riding the wild country in Utah is Robert Redford, an expert horseman, which no doubt helped him some in movies like *Butch Cassidy and the Sundance Kid.* He is also an avid skier (which he practiced in the film *Downhill Racer*) and owner of a ski resort complex in Utah.

▲ The Strip in Las Vegas is an odd setting for a basketball game, but Bill Cosby takes his exercise where he can get it. He did not make the shot, perhaps because he wasn't looking at the basket. ▶ Another hoopster, Dinah Shore, lets one fly in the backyard of her Beverly Hills home in 1960, and unlike Bill Cosby she has her eye on the basket. Looking on is Dinah's husband, George Montgomery, who seems to have his sports mixed up.

The "Schnoz," Jimmy Durante, with characteristic cigar, fishes from the California shore with
friend Desi Arnaz in 1958. In his gravelly voice
he has just told Arnaz that "Nobody outfishes
Durante!"

As comfortable on the golf course as he is with a good joke, Bob Hope blasts one during the 1962 Desert Classic in Palm Springs.

Needless to say, the putt Jackie Gleason just tapped rolled into the hole.

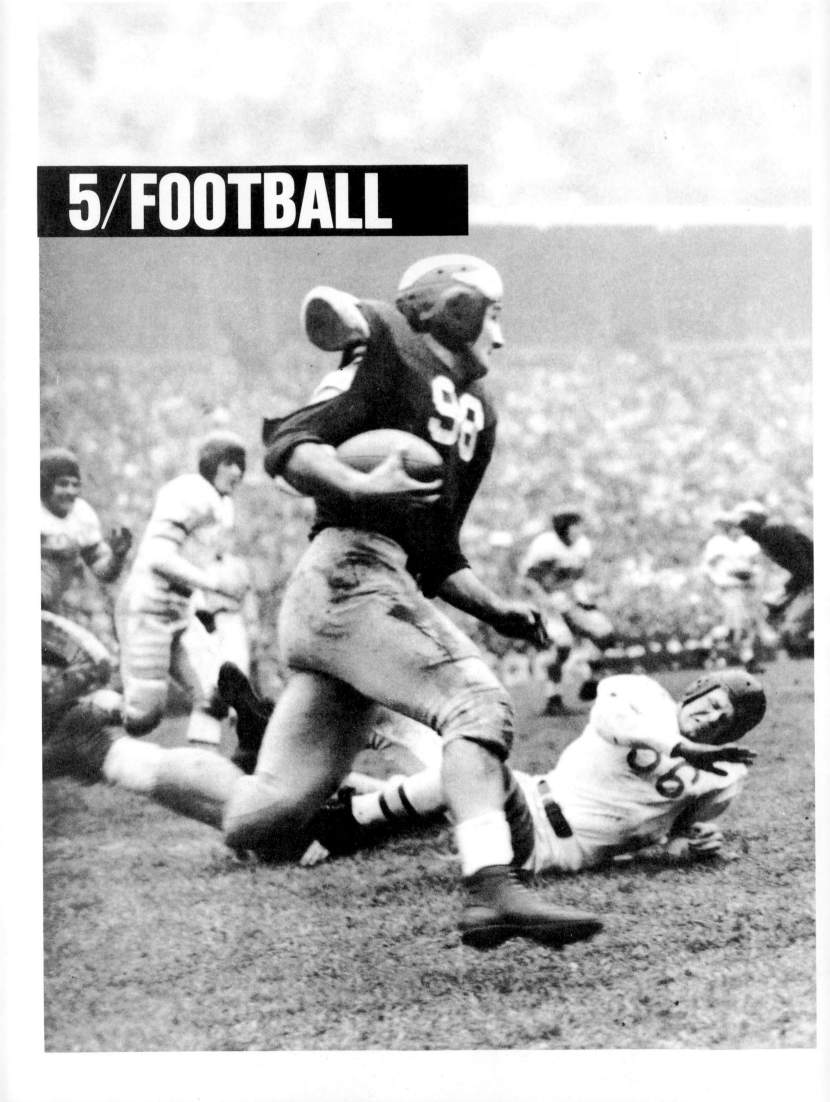

5/FOOTBALL

◄ This famous photo of Tom Harmon, his jersey ravaged and his eye on the goal line, was taken in his last college game. The Michigan star, winner of the Heisman Trophy that year, 1940, scored three touchdowns in the game against Ohio State to break two collegiate records that had been held since 1925 by Red Grange: career touchdowns (33 to Grange's 31) and career points scored (237 to Grange's 186).

▲ Dana Xenophon Bible with his Texas team of 1941, which he felt might bring him a national championship. Bible, a stern disciplinarian and true to his name, was noted for quoting Scripture to his ballplayers. He was a head coach from 1913 through 1946, the last 10 years of which were spent at Texas. This "wonder team," as they were dubbed, ended up fourth in the national rankings for 1941.

▲ The dream backfield if ever there was one, Army of 1945: *(from the left)* halfback Shorty McWilliams, quarterback Arnold Tucker, fullback Doc Blanchard, and halfback Glenn Davis. The three Army powerhouses that featured Blanchard and Davis, Mr. Inside and Mr. Outside, 1944–1946, never lost a game and tied only one (Notre Dame in 1946). ◄ Bill Stern, foremost sportscaster of his time, chats with All-American quarterback Johnny Lujack in the Notre Dame locker room. Lujack led the Fighting Irish to a national championship the year this photo appeared in *Life*, 1946, and was awarded the Heisman Trophy the next year.

Army's coach Earl Blaik had plenty to smile about in 1946, at least until he ran into Notre Dame a little later in the season. He is pictured here with back Shorty McWilliams, who was a kind of cause célèbre himself that year because he had tried to quit Army and go back to Mississippi State where he had played in 1944. West Point's superintendent, Major General Maxwell Taylor, refused to let him resign, but after a lot of ink and talk about McWilliams being a "prisoner of the academy," he was allowed to leave the school.

A scene from one of the most famous college football games of all time, Army–Notre Dame, 1946. Here Doc Blanchard goes high in the air to snare a pass from Glenn Davis and then was knocked out of bounds at the Notre Dame 23. But Army was unable to get the ball across the goal line that day, as was Notre Dame, and the two titans of college football played to a scoreless tie.

▲ One of the most elusive runners of the late 1940s, Charlie "Choo Choo" Justice of North Carolina, putting a move on a would-be tackler here, was called in 1949 "the most famous southerner since Robert E. Lee." ◄ Kyle Rote, carrying the ball here against Texas, was the chief reason Southern Methodist was ranked No. 1 in the nation going into this 1950 game. The talented tailback, an heir to the All-American slot vacated by Doak Walker, who graduated from SMU the year before, could not get his Mustangs going, however, and they were upset by Texas 23–20.

◀ After their dramatic meeting in 1952, Notre Dame's famed coach Frank Leahy *(left)* congratulates Michigan State's Biggie Munn. No. 3 ranked Notre Dame had maintained hopes of knocking off the top-ranked Spartans, but Irish ball-carriers fumbled seven times and they lost 21–3. It was the Spartans' twenty-third consecutive victory. But Leahy's disappointment would fade the following year when his green and gold Irish shared the college football crown with Maryland, and on that note he retired as Notre Dame's winningest coach (107 wins, 13 losses, 9 ties).

◀ Several decades before Monday night football, Frank Gifford romped on the playing field for Southern Cal as he (16) is doing here on a 69-yard touchdown run against California in 1951. As a result, USC was able to upset No. 1 ranked Cal 21–14 in a game that was variously described as the "upset of the year" and the "most brutally spectacular game of the 1951 season."

▼ Bringing back memories of the 60-minute men, Notre Dame's quarterback in 1954, Ralph Guglielmi, starts back with a pass he has just intercepted in his additional role as a defensive back. The upended player is Texas end Howard Moon, the intended receiver. Notre Dame won it 21–0, their first game under new coach Terry Brennan.

Hulking across the field is Detroit Lion rookie tackle Alex Karras, forced to take a few laps for horsing around in practice. After his illustrious career in the NFL, Karras horsed around as the Neanderthal Mungo in Mel Brooks's movie *Blazing Saddles,* his most memorable scene being when he slugs a horse and knocks it out.

Army great Pete Dawkins cradles the ball and smiles for the camera in Notre Dame's end zone with one of two touchdowns the cadets scored to beat the Fighting Irish 14–2 in 1958, the first time Army had defeated Notre Dame since the Blanchard-Davis era in the mid-1940s. Dawkins was a consensus All-American and the Heisman Trophy winner that year.

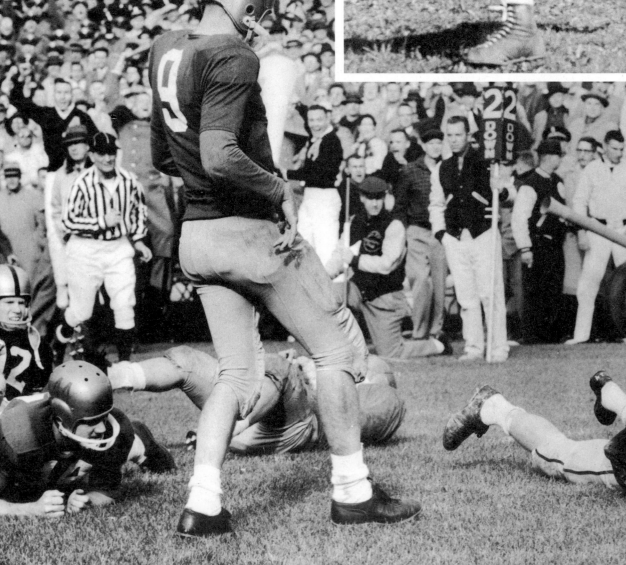

▲ It ordinarily took about this many tacklers to subdue Cleveland Browns fullback Jim Brown. The three New York Giants gang-tackling him in this 1958 game are Cliff Livingston (89), Andy Robustelli (81), and Jim Patton (20). And moving in to help is Rosey Grier (76).

▶ Baltimore Colts' Big Daddy Lipscomb, 6 feet 7 inches and somewhere around 300 pounds, has designs on removing the head of Detroit Lions quarterback Earl Morrall in this 1959 game. About Big Daddy's style of defensive play coach Weeb Ewbank said, "He sorts the backs out and when he comes to the ball carrier, that's the one he keeps."

◄ His head seemingly embedded in the ground, Pittsburgh Steeler end Buddy Dial gives solid testimony that pain and suffering are part of the pro game. Hovering behind him is New York Giant defensive back Lindon Crow.

▼ Navy's Joe Bellino carries a passel of Notre Dame tacklers in 1960 and he also scored two touchdowns to give the midshipmen a 14–7 victory in that game. After Bellino led Navy to a 10–1 season and a ranking in the nation's top ten teams, an official at the Naval Academy said of the Heisman Trophy winner, "If Bellino stays in the Navy with that record he'll be the greatest Italian admiral since Christopher Columbus."

▲ This unique-angle photo of a Baltimore Colt kickoff in 1960 appeared on the cover of *Life* and won first prize in the sports category of the prestigious "News Pictures of the Year" contest for staffer George Silk. The Colts in the picture are Johnny Sample (44), Steve Myrha (65), and Sherman Plunkett.

▶ Johnny Unitas, the great Baltimore Colt quarterback of the 1960s, liked to stay in the pocket and throw at the very last instant. Sometimes he waited a little too long. The pass rusher about to weld Unitas to the turf is Earl Leggett of the Chicago Bears.

The New York Giants of the late 1950s and early 1960s were an extraordinary team. For a while they had as their two chief assistant coaches Vince Lombardi to handle the offense and Tom Landry the defense. From 1956 through 1963, they won six eastern conference championships.

The Giants defense of that era has become legendary: the linemen included the likes of Andy Robustelli, Rosey Grier, Dick Modzelewski, and Jim Katcavage; linebackers such as Sam Huff, Harland Svare, and Cliff Livingston; defensive backs the caliber of Emlen Tunnell, Jim Patton, Lindon Crow, Erich Barnes, and Dick Lynch. On offense there were such venerables in the backfield as Charlie Conerly, Y. A. Tittle, Frank Gifford, Mel Triplett, Alex Webster, and Joe Morrison; pass catchers like Kyle Rote and Del Shofner; blockers with reputations like Rosey Brown, Ray Wietecha, and Greg Larson. All were guided first by head coach Jim Lee Howell and later by Allie Sherman.

The Giants were a spectacle to behold, a dynasty by sports definition. *Life* recorded them in action and transcribed all the violence and power in a photo essay in 1960.

► Rushing Philadelphia Eagle punter Norm Van Brocklin (11) are linebackers Cliff Livingston (89) and Sam Huff (70).

▼ The Giant defense moves in to try to stop high-diving fullback John Olszewski of the Washington Redskins. No. 66 is Jack Stroud.

That's the Giant's Frank Gifford *(dark jersey)* being manhandled by the Eagles' perennial All-Pro Chuck Bednarik.

▲ Not a bad array of quarterbacks in the NFL in 1961. They range from grizzled veterans like Y. A. Tittle, 35 years old, and Bobby Layne, 34, to such youngsters as Norm Snead, 21, and Dandy Don Meredith, 23.

▶ Ara Parseghian reacts with anguish as his football world crumbles in the last minute of Notre Dame's last game of the 1964 season when a rallying Southern Cal scored a touchdown to win the game 20–17. Parseghian, in his first year as head coach, had brought his Fighting Irish through nine games without a defeat and had his eye on the national championship, but it all slipped away in the final moments of this game. No. 7 is ND's quarterback John Huarte and 31 is fullback Joe Kantor.

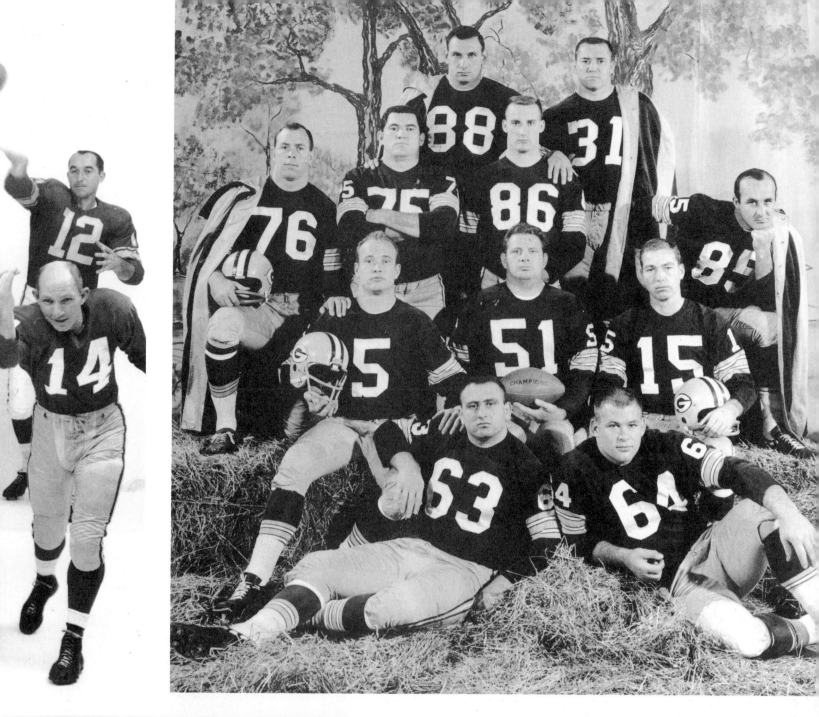

▲ The magnificient Pack of Green Bay pose on a haystack in 1962, looking as regal as the crownbearers they in fact were: bottom row, guards Fuzzy Thurston and Jerry Kramer; second row, halfback Paul Hornung, center Jim Ringo, quarterback Bart Starr; third row, tackles Bob Skoronski and Forrest Gregg, flanker Boyd Dowler, end Max McGee; top row, end Ron Kramer, fullback Jim Taylor. The Packers lost only one game that year, then whipped the New York Giants 16–7 for the NFL title.

◄ A pair of Notre Dame's staunchest football fans.

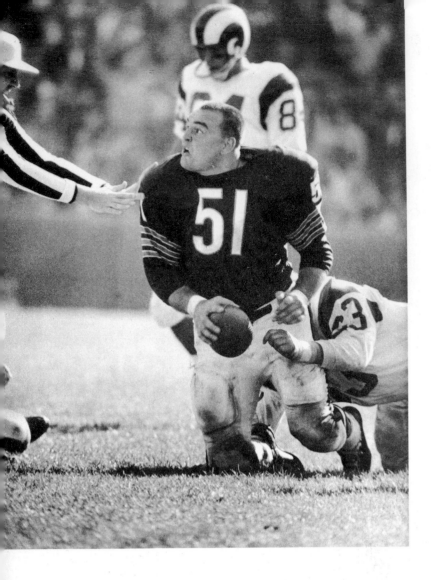

Dick Butkus, rookie middle linebacker for the Chicago Bears in 1965, shows more than a trace of displeasure after a Los Angeles Ram player ripped off his helmet by the facemask. It took only a game or two for word to spread through the NFL about what a savage and dominating force Butkus was on a football field, and in his first season he was named All-Pro.

The scrambler, Fran Tarkenton of the Minnesota Vikings, is undeterred by Chicago Bear Doug Atkins, who appears to be trying to tear his leg off. "I only scramble in an emergency," Tarkenton said. Perhaps he should have added, or when I am not in the clutches of a ravenous 6-feet 8-inch 260-pound defensive end.

Everyone chases Green Bay's Paul Hornung (5) through a late autumn rain, but it's futile as he carries in a Bart Starr pass for his fifth touchdown of the day. The Packers demolished the Baltimore Colts 42–27 and went on to win the NFL championship.

The pain and numbing fatigue of playing pro football when you're 35 years old is personified by a mud-soaked Dick Modzelewski of the Cleveland Browns. "Charlie Conerly used to say it's time to quit if you're still sore on Sunday from the last game," Modzelewski explained. "Now the soreness doesn't leave me until Friday. This leaves me one day—maybe another year before I quit."

113

▶ In a special *Life* essay on members of the NFC champion Baltimore Colts of 1968, Ogden Nash versified this caption to describe the mountainous Bubba Smith (78):

> When hearing tales of Bubba Smith
> You wonder is he man or myth.
> He's like a hoodoo, like a hex,
> He's like Tyrannosaurus Rex.
> Few manage to topple in a tussle
> Three hundred pounds of
>   hustle and muscle.
> He won't complain if double-teamed;
> It isn't Bubba who gets creamed.
> What gained this pair of underminers?
> Only four Forty-niner shiners.

◀ Broadway Joe Namath, notorious for his wobbly knees, feels one of them giving way as he tries to fend off Ike Lassiter of the Oakland Raiders in a 1968 game. But the knees held up enough to enable Namath to lead the New York Jets to Super Bowl III, where they became the first AFC team to win that classic.

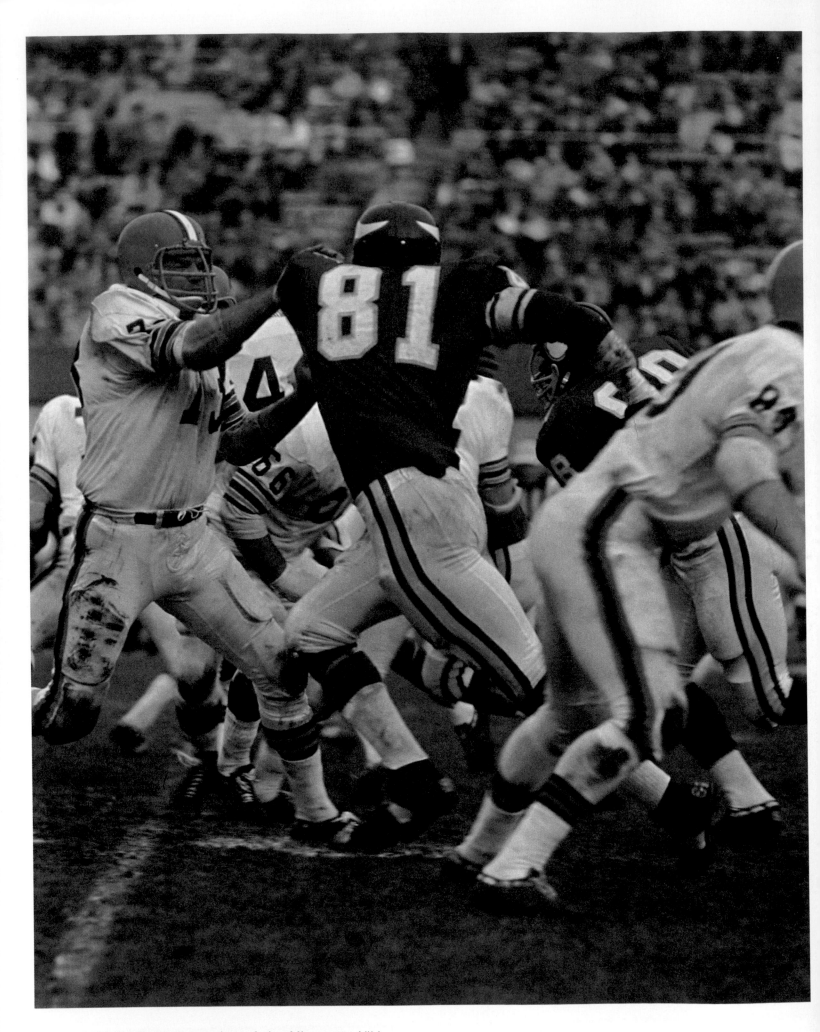

Violence at the front: a member of the Minnesota Vikings
Purple Gang, defensive end Carl Eller (81), charges the Detroit
offensive line. The fabled Purple Gang coined a motto for
themselves: ''Meet at the quarterback.''

Running backs were a vital force in the NFL in 1972. Here four of the best tell what they think of the game and their roles in it in a *Life* essay that year.

O. J. Simpson of the Buffalo Bills. "I'm not a punishing type of runner. . . . But I never let a defender get a good shot at me. When I was in college I never tried to fake a linebacker in the first quarter—I'd just hit him as hard as I could, even when I didn't have the ball."

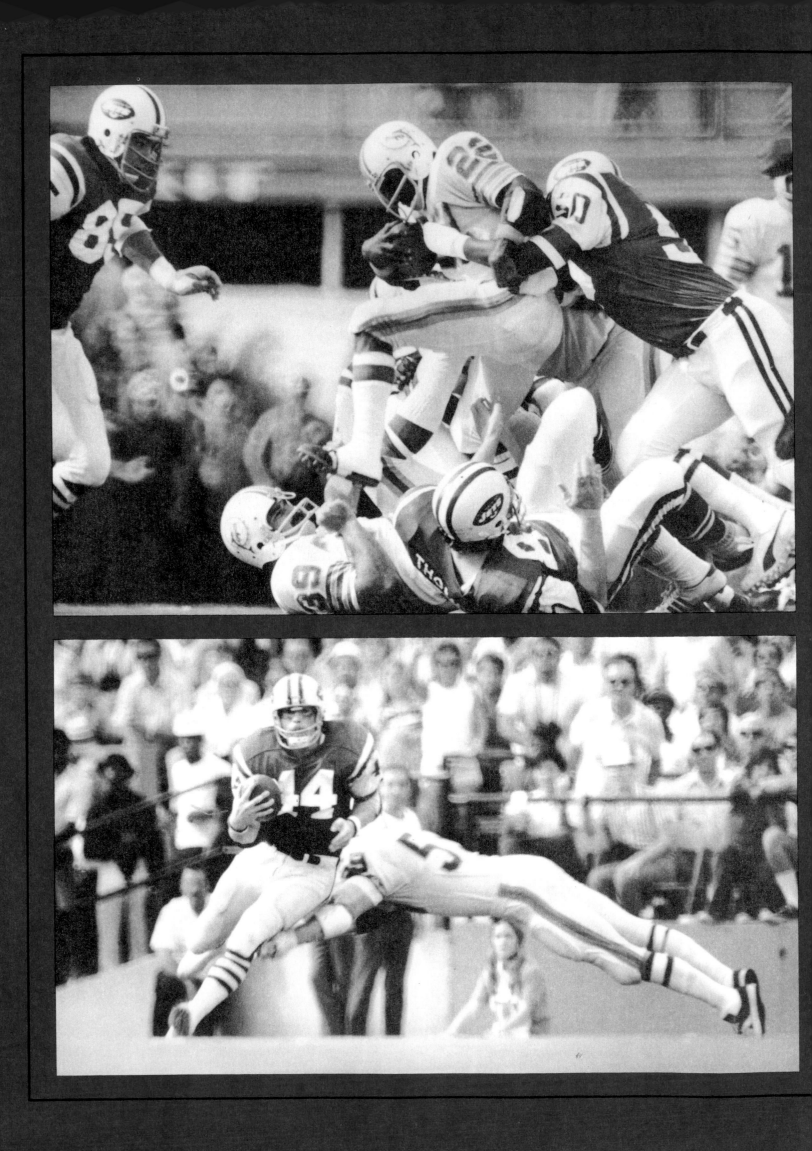

◄John Riggins of the New York Jets. "I'm not a breakaway runner, but I've got more power. And I like to block. I like going downfield and hunting out a man to knock down." ►Larry Czonka of the Miami Dolphins. "Here I am with my tenth broken nose because I'm always getting knocked around. . . . I am an up-the-middle man—but it hurts a whole lot." ◄Mercury Morris of the Miami Dolphins. "A lot of backs complain about the pounding their legs take from the artificial turf. Not me, I like it. It's like running in the street—and that's where I learned to play."

6/RACES AND RACERS

In one of the most memorable 100-meter dashes of all time, Barney Ewell *(second from the left)* breaks the tape a step ahead of favorite and holder of the world's record for the 100-yard dash, Mel Patton *(far left)*. The race took place at the 1948 Olympic trials at Northwestern's Dyche Stadium in Evanston, Illinois, and Ewell's time of 10.2 tied the world's record. In the lane between Patton and Ewell, Bill Mathis is beginning a tumble that will send him skidding into the cinders. The other sprinters are, from the right, Don Campbell, Harrison Dillard, and Eddie Conwell.

◀The streaking greyhound, covering 16 feet with each bounding stride and capable of reaching speeds in excess of 35 miles per hour, is caught in all the tension and fury of its motion by Gjon Mili's high-speed camera, which he had half-buried in the middle of the track, tripping the shutter from his off-track position. The photo of the 2-year-old racer named River Border was taken at Boston's Wonderland Park in 1948.

▼ A view of the wide-ranging sport of harness racing, whose origins go back to England circa 1750. This photo captures the race in its rural character, a tradition at state and county fairs since early in the nineteenth century; this especially picturesque scene was played out at Connersville, Indiana in 1956 where tickets cost $1 and the only gambling allowed was "a $1 man-to-man bet."

The fastest and most potentially dangerous of all winter sports is ice boat racing, sometimes called ice yachting, although that title imparts a kind of serenity and leisure to it that are truly not a part of this sport. Dutch settlers in the eighteenth century were the first to combine sailboat and skis, essentially for the sake of transportation, and let the wintry winds power them across lakes or down rivers that were thickly frozen. In the twentieth century the same type of craft are used for sport: "racing for the exceptionally hardy, cold-weather types," as one observer put it.

The lightweight, highly maneuverable craft usually travel over prescribed courses (often marked only by old Christmas trees) at speeds of 60 to 80 miles per hour, but the more proficient can attain speeds of over 100. In fact, the world's record according to Guinness is 143 miles an hour, set by John T. Buckstaff on Lake Winnebago, Wisconsin, in 1938.

The races are dramatic, with the whip-crack sound of wind snapping into sail and the screech of metal runners as they rocket across the ice. The wind and the cold are arctically intimidating and the hazards are everywhere, from snowbanks and Christmas tree markers to patches of thin ice to collisions and capsizings. It was this cold and lonely setting in Wisconsin and the daring winter sportsmen who enjoy it that enticed *Life* photographer George Silk, who more customarily photographed sailing on the more traditional water, to do this essay in 1962.

▼ Some racers scorn ski masks like this thick-skinned pilot. Some say they like the feel of the wind in their faces, unawed by polar wind-chill factors, frostbite, and needle-sharp chips of ice that are churned up by the boat's forward runner.

▲ This ice boat racer, close-hauled to the wind, hits a snowdrift but manages to keep control of his streaking craft. The plank holding the runner, shown at the lower left, is built so that it will bend with the craft's vibrations to absorb some of the shock. Class E ice boats like this one are about 22 feet in length, weigh about 500 pounds, and carry 75 square feet of sail, and can reach speeds twice that of the winds that power them. ▼ In all its icy action, a race is caught at one of its most perilous moments, as two boats' sails catch a puff of wind and begin "hiking." That is, in the jargon of the sport, when the windward runner is off the ice, tilting boat and pilot into an airplanelike bank. If a pilot doesn't take immediate corrective action by turning closer into the wind, the hike can turn into a capsize, not a pleasant experience at 80 or so miles an hour. Still, ice boat racers say there is nothing more thrilling in the sport than gliding on a single runner.

◄ *Life* was at the 1938 Boston Marathon and captured the drama of it, climaxed when Leslie Pawson, 33 years old and a native of Pawtucket, Rhode Island, crossed the finish line first with a time of 2 hours, 35 minutes, 34 seconds.

▼ In one of the great mile match-ups of the time, Gene Fenske (Wisconsin) passes Glenn Cunningham (Kansas) in the 1940 national indoor championship at Madison Square Garden. Cunningham, who had held the world record for the mile from 1934 to 1937 (4:06.8), stumbled and fell moments later. Trailing the two is another premier miler, Gene Venske.

Two of the best milers of the late 1940s, the Reverend Gil Dodds and Don Gehrmann. ◄ Dodds, 29 years old and a preacher for the First Brethren Church, is in the process here of breaking the world's indoor mile record at the 1948 Millrose Games in New York City with a time of 4:05.3. ▼ Gehrmann, shown winning the Millrose Games mile the following year with a time of 4:09.5, was only a junior at the University of Wisconsin in 1949.

◄ An ignominious moment for the world's best high hurdler occurred at the 1948 Olympic trials. Harrison Dillard of Baldwin-Wallace College comes to a complete halt and disqualification at the seventh hurdle in the 110-meter hurdle trial after having knocked over four of the preceding hurdles. It was the same Harrison Dillard who, a few months earlier, had broken the world's record in the same event. But all was not lost because Dillard qualified for the 100-meter dash that year, went to London, and brought back the Olympic gold medal in that event. Four years later he would take the gold in the 110-meter hurdles and not knock down a single one in the effort.

► One of track and field's landmark barriers falls as Roger Bannister breaks the tape, becoming the first man ever to run the mile in less than 4 minutes. The 25-year-old medical student did it here at his alma mater, Oxford, in 1954; he posted a time of 3:59.4 and then collapsed into the arms of well-wishers.

It was headlined "The Greatest Mile Race in History," and in 1954 it was indeed just that. As *Life* reported, "When England's Roger Bannister ran it in 3:59.4 last May 6, sportswriters thought his record might endure for years. It lasted six weeks; on June 21 Australia's John Landy did it in 3:58 flat. From that instant, a race between Bannister and Landy loomed as the greatest individual contest of the twentieth century."

The race was set for August, the setting the British Empire Games in Vancouver, British Columbia. There were a swarm of timekeepers to be sure the race was properly clocked and a myriad of reporters and photographers to appropriately record the historic confrontation. No one seemed to know or care who the other six milers in the race were. All that mattered were the Englishman and the Australian who had broken the 4-minute-mile barrier.

Word spread that Bannister, seen tending to his sniffles just before the start of the race, was suffering from a cold that afternoon. Landy, on the other hand, was detached, a study in concentration and introspection. But all that was forgotten with the report of the starter's pistol.

▼ Landy, deciding to set the pace, jumps to an early lead. Bannister, holding back in his traditional pattern, is in fifth place at the end of the first quarter mile. ▶ As they come into the stretch, Bannister makes his move and Landy looks to find him, but sees nothing but empty track behind him.

Bannister's closing sprint is insurmountable and, with the agony of the effort captured here, he reaches the tape a full 6 yards ahead of Landy. The British team manager, Leslie Truelove, rushed out to catch the collapsing Bannister. The race lived up to expectations, with both runners coming in under 4 minutes—Bannister 3:58.8 and Landy 3:59.6.

Jim Beatty, racing for the Los Angeles Track Club at a meet in New York, runs to a new world's indoor mile record of 3:58.6 in 1963. "The original idea was to run to win, not run for good time," Beatty said afterwards. "But I wanted to be the first guy to go under four minutes in the Garden." And so he was.

The world's most highly regarded miler in 1958, the barefoot Australian Herb Elliott *(left)* works out with his 63-year-old coach Percy Cerutty. Cerutty, who took up marathoning at age 44, evidently has found a certain ecstasy in the sport. Elliott set a new world's record for the mile that year, 3:54.5, and ran it in under 4 minutes numerous times. According to coach Cerutty, "We're just two blokes trying to accomplish something together. I'm the older bloke with experience. He's the younger bloke who can learn a bit and use it beating those other fellows."

A unique triple exposure from the camera of *Life* photographer Ralph Morse narrates the story of the 60-yard dash at the 1956 Millrose Games in New York. The sprinters are photographed at the start, middle, and finish, a span of time of about 6.2 seconds. And the story of the race was that John Haines *(second from right)* of Pennsylvania got out of the blocks a shade slowly but surged ahead to beat a field of fine sprinters: from the left, Brooks Johnson of Tufts, Ken Kave of Morgan State, Andy Stanfield of the New York Pioneer Club and *(to the right of Haines)* Willie Williams of the U.S. Army.

George Silk's camera bends and forms this hurdling trio into a fluid, precision ballet. The symmetrical tandem is formed by Willie May, Hayes Jones, and Lee Calhoun. The three were photographed separately as each went over his hurdle at a 1960 meet.

Dust racing, it is called; and a smothering 400-mile venture across a dust-choked desert near Las Vegas is what this masked driver is undertaking. The basic requirement for entering the race is a four-wheel vehicle—dune buggies, jeeps, pickups, sedans, and elaborate variations thereof all appear at the starting line. This race began at 9 A.M. and lasted until 1 A.M. the next day. The talcumlike dust was so thick and deep during one stretch that many of the racers bogged down and had to be towed out. As one of them put it, "The dust comes over you like a solid wall of water." Of the 264 entries only 26 finished the race, with the winner averaging perhaps the toughest 30 miles per hour in auto racing.

The dash, daring, and drama of the steeplechase are captured in this remarkable, award-winning photo taken at a competition in the English countryside in 1960. The riders, etched against the sky, are, according to *Life*, at "the most electrifying moment in a harrowing sport [which] comes when steeplechasers soar toward the highest fence. The wind whistles, the hooves hammer, the riders curse—and occasionally mixed in is the ominous thump of flesh and bone against unyielding birch."

▲ A spectacle of dust and noise as an exceptionally large and densely packed motorcycle race gets under way. More than 650 dust-masked cyclists met in the spring of 1971 to race 75 miles across California's Mojave Desert. On the carpet of sand and dust some motorcyclists reached speeds of 85 miles per hour.

◄ Out to break the world's motorcycle speed record, Roland Free, a filling station operator, roars across the Bonneville Salt Flats in Utah in 1948. He balanced himself flat on the rear fender to reduce the drag from wind friction, reached a speed of 150.855 miles an hour for a new record, and managed to stay on the cycle over the entire 1-mile course.

Drag racing, an infatuation in America after World War II, was illegal in most localities and was frowned upon by all but the teenagers involved even when it was legal, which was the case with this meet at Santa Ana, California, in 1957. More than 3000 spectators lined up their own hot rods on the flanks of the course and 358 participated in the races.

The perils of motorcycle racing are horrifyingly dramatized in this flip-out at an amateur 100-mile race at Daytona Beach, Florida, in 1948. The catapulted driver was one of 30 injured in the race around a 4.1-mile beach and macadam track.

George Silk took this panoramic picture from a helicopter at a twenty-fifth anniversary regatta on Lake Erie staged by owners of Thistle sailboats (17-foot racing dinghys) in 1970. Silk also sailed his own Thistle, but usually on Long Island Sound.

Whirlaway, grand thoroughbred that he was, ordinarily was pressed a little more than in this
anomaly of a race in 1942. He is about to win
with ease a $10,000 purse at a Baltimore race-
track because all the other horses had been
withdrawn before the race. Much of the reason
undoubtedly was the fact that Whirlaway had
won the Triple Crown (Kentucky Derby, Preak-
ness, Belmont Stakes) the year before.

One of horse racing's greatest jockeys, Willie Hartack seems less than exuberant on the occasion of his 400th victory of 1956. At 23 here, he had yet to win a Kentucky Derby, although he would win five in the years to come. Still, as one trainer observed, "They'd bet [on Hartack] if he was riding Mrs. O'Leary's cow."

On the occasion in 1952 of riding his 4000th winner, jockey Johnny Longden, instead of the horse, is draped with a victory blanket of white carnations and red camellias. With him is his son Vance, a veterinarian. At the time the next winningest jockey in the history of the sport had about a thousand fewer than Longden. When Longden finally hung up his silks, he had won a total of 6032 races.

A classic consultation. Sunny Jim Fitzsimmons, trainer of the great Nashua, tells jockey Eddie Arcaro, just before the heralded $100,000 match race between Nashua and Swaps at Chicago's Washington Park in 1955, "I've done all I can do. You're the engineer now." Between the two they did it well because Nashua was an easy winner that afternoon.

7/CUPS, BOWLS, AND OTHER SPORTS CLASSICS

The start of the 1959 Kentucky Derby is caught in this panoramic photo because *Life's* George Silk mounted a Panon camera atop the starting gate. The lens, set in a movable turret, turns in an arc across stationary film after being triggered, exposing everything in a 140-degree range. When the classic mile and a quarter was run, the bunch so even here had thinned out considerably, but two noses reached the finish line almost simultaneously, Tomy Lee (8, his jockey with a "T" on the back of his shirt) and Sword Dancer (10). The photo finish showed Tomy Lee, with Willie Shoemaker aboard, barely a nostril ahead.

Even a certified mudder wouldn't venture onto the track on this January day at Churchill Downs in 1937. The hauntingly beautiful photograph was taken by Margaret Bourke-White shortly after the Ohio River surged over its banks and flooded Louisville, Kentucky. Five months later, with the floodwaters gone, the track dry and dusty, America's great racing tradition continued as the Kentucky Derby was held right on schedule. It was won by the indomitable War Admiral, who then went on to win the Triple Crown, becoming only the fourth horse in history to do so.

Two chapters in the story of how Australia snatched the Davis Cup from the United States in 1950 are dramatized in these scenes from Forest Hills. ▶Aussie Frank Sedgman *(far court)* drives a cross-court volley past Tom Brown of the U.S. for one of the points along the way to his singles triumph. ▼In the doubles match, it is Sedgman *(near court)* again, this time about to drive a volley at the feet of America's Gardner Mulloy. Sedgman's partner is Jack Bromwich and Mulloy's is Ted Schroeder, in what turned out to be a breathtakingly suspenseful match in which the Australians eventually prevailed (4–6, 6–4, 6–2, 4–6, 6–4).

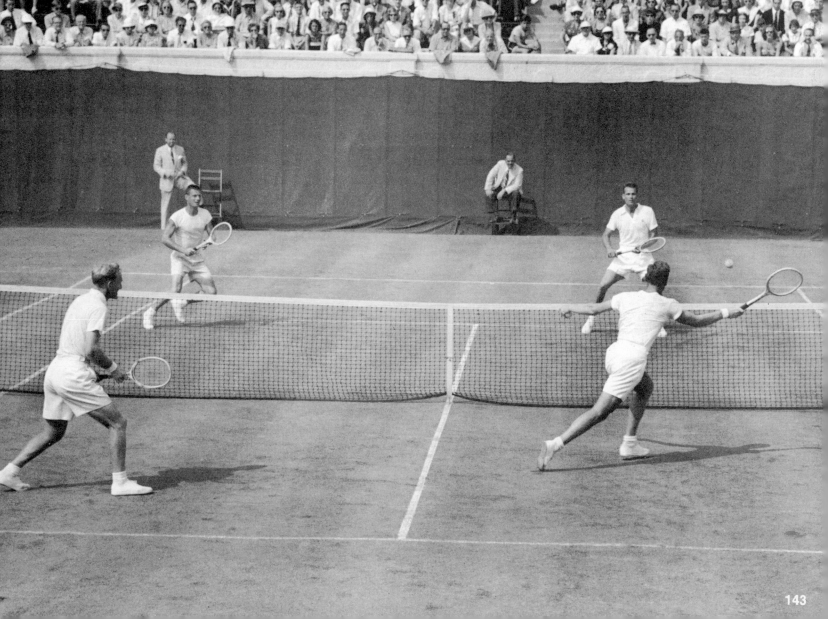

◄ Wallace Triplett of Penn State, sweeping the end with a touch of acrobatics here, was one of two blacks on the Nittany Lions, not only the first to play in the Cotton Bowl classic, but actually the first to play in an interracial sports contest in Texas. The year was 1948 and, as *Life* noted, "some fans booed." But Triplett was undeterred and scored a touchdown that New Year's afternoon to help Penn State tie a favored, Doak Walker-led Southern Methodist, 13–13.   ▼ All eyes are on Michigan end Bob Mann as he cradles a pass from All-American Bob Chappuis in the Rose Bowl match-up against Southern Cal on New Year's Day 1948. The Wolverines were the top team in the nation in 1947, and they left little doubt of their ranking in Pasadena when they annihilated USC 49–0.

▲ There is more than a trace of anxiety on Sam Snead's face as he chips onto the green in the final round of the 1952 Masters tournament at Augusta, Georgia. Going into the round he and Ben Hogan were dead even at 214 after three rounds. But Slammin' Sam was steady and sure and carried off the $20,000 first prize. ▶ Despite a withered left arm, Ed Furgol still could play with the world's best golfers, as he proved at the 1954 U.S. Open. He won the prestigious tournament, bettering such legends of the links as Ben Hogan and Sam Snead. Handicapped since he broke the arm at age 11, Furgol's power was generated by his right arm and by rotating his upper torso in an unorthodox fashion; as he put it, "by doing everything that, as a country club pro, I tell my students not to do."

Sitting down on the job in the 1953 World Series are Junior Gilliam of the Brooklyn Dodgers *(left)* and Phil Rizzuto of the New York Yankees. Actually Gilliam had tried to steal second and Rizzuto tagged him out, then turned his back not in scorn but to toss the ball to a teammate. The Yanks took the Series that year, their fifth in a row.

"Cutting the Waves for a Classic Cup" is the way *Life* headlined a spectacular photo essay of the spray-filled, savagely contested competition among four 12-meter sloops—*Nefertiti, Weatherly, Easterner,* and *Columbia*—to represent the United States in the 1962 America's Cup race. Staffer George Silk brought his camera and his unbound imagination aboard all four racing yachts to record the action of the trial races off Newport, Rhode Island.

When it was over, *Weatherly* had earned the honor to bear the standard for the United States against Australia's highly regarded challenger *Gretel.* And for the nineteenth consecutive time since the Cup was conceived in 1851, the United States emerged victorious, as *Weatherly* carried on the grand tradition.

▼ A uniquely angled shot catches the polished bow of *Easterner* as it knifes through the Atlantic waters. To get this extraordinary photo, Silk fastened his feet under a rail, ignored the rush of water and hull beneath him, and positioned himself to snap the bow as it plowed a swath through the ocean.

The port rail of *Weatherly* is almost engulfed by the sea and the crew clings to the starboard for counterbalance. All but one, that is, and he, undisturbed and deftly balanced, intently checks the jib trim.

The tension, concentration, and downright exhausting labor of crewing in a major race is preserved forever in the portrait of this sailor on *Nefertiti* as he works the "coffee grinder."

For this dramatic photo, Silk climbed to the top of *Nefertiti*'s 88-foot mast. From that precarious perch, he captures the sloop's huge red-topped spinnaker as it bellies out in light air, as well as the crew working cohesively at their varied tasks on deck. Crewman number six, incidentally, is lying on the deck in order to get a better view of the spinnaker's leading edge so he can check trim.

▲ Dusty Rhodes (left) follows teammates Hank Thompson (far right) and Willie Mays around the bases after clubbing a pinch-hit home run to win the first game of the 1954 World Series for the New York Giants. Tossing his glove in the air in disgust is Cleveland Indian pitcher Bob Lemon; the catcher is Jim Hegan. The Giants swept the Series in four straight. ◄ Jackie Robinson taunted pitchers with animated lead-offs like this when he ran the bases for the Brooklyn Dodgers in the late 1940s and early 1950s. And if they didn't take the taunting seriously, he might just steal home, as he daringly starts to do here in the 1955 World Series. A moment later, he slid safely under the pitch from Whitey Ford to Yogi Berra to help Brooklyn win the first game of the Series and ultimately their first world championship.

Willie Mays makes his historic catch in the 1954 World Series to rob Cleveland Indian slugger Vic Wertz of an extra-base hit with two runners on base. At the crack of the bat, Mays turned and raced until he finally got his glove on the ball 450 feet from home plate.

Dodger left fielder Sandy Amoros makes a sensational catch to rob Yogi Berra of what appeared to be a sure extra-base hit in the seventh and final game of the 1955 World Series. Amoros then fired the ball to Pee Wee Reese who relayed it to Gil Hodges to double Gil McDougald off first base and thoroughly stifle a Yankee rally. That's McDougald standing on second base at the moment he realizes that Amoros has made a remarkable catch.

301 FT.

A weary and pained Ben Hogan trudges uphill to the seventh green during the 1955 U.S. Open. He is pressing on his thighs to ease the pain in his left knee, which was badly damaged in an automobile accident in 1949, one that almost ended Hogan's golf career. At the moment this picture was taken, Hogan was leading the field, but a relative unknown by the name of Jack Fleck came on to tie him in the final round. The strain of the playoff was too much for Hogan, and Fleck won it. But Hogan had four other U.S. Open titles to console himself with, the most any golfer has ever won (a record he shares with Willie Anderson, Bobby Jones, and Jack Nicklaus).

The most astonishing performance of the 1956 World Series was delivered by Don Larsen, who pitched perfect baseball for the Yankees in game five. Twenty-seven Dodger batters faced the flawless right-hander and not one of them reached first base. Larsen threw only 97 pitches during his perfect no-hitter, a feat never before nor since accomplished in World Series play. Here he is shown serving up one of those 97 pitches.

▶ Slashing through the waters over the historic yachting course of the America's Cup race, a hopeful crew guides *Vim* in a practice run. The sleek 12-meter racing sloop was one of four yachts that vied to represent the United States in 1958 against England's entry *Sceptre*. *Vim,* however, lost out in the trials to *Columbia*.

In its moment of ultimate victory, a blanketed Iron Liege is led from the track by a Calumet Farms exercise boy after the colt's unexpected win in the eighty-third Kentucky Derby in 1957. Willie Hartack rode Iron Liege to a photo-finish triumph, but neither would have been in the winner's circle had not Willie Shoemaker mistakenly stood in the stirrups and slowed Gallant Man down as the two horses raced toward the finish line.

AMERICA'S CUP RACES BIGGEST SHOW ON SEAS

A portion of the Atlantic Ocean off Newport, Rhode Island, last week was congested by one of the largest peacetime flotillas in history. The boats, lured by the spectacle of the first America's Cup defense in 21 years, had gathered from both sides of the Atlantic and as far west as Texas, flying every kind of burgee. The owners were smartly decked out in yachting caps, their wives in fur wraps and sneakers. Guests sipped happily at drinks.

The spectator fleet, some 2000 boats strong, surrounded and overshadowed the two contestants all along the course. Here at the half point of the first race, America's defender, Columbia (right above), had rounded the marker while Britain's underdog challenger, Sceptre, was still sailing the opposite way. Back and forth on a course paralleling that of the racers, harbor tugs and tiny runabouts rubbed gunwales on palatial yachts and luxury liners. Sprinkled among them were British, American, and Canadian warships, including a destroyer with President Eisenhower on board. When the race became close, as it did briefly in the second leg, the rubberneck fleet reacted by stepping up its pace. Big yachts and outboard jalopies bounced harder and higher on each other's wake, putting paint jobs and tempers in jeopardy. When the one-sided race was over, with Columbia winning by almost 8 minutes, the combined horns and sirens of the entire fleet sounded an ear-shattering nautical salute.

Besides wanting to be a witness to yachting's most hallowed competition, most of the visitors were bent on a saltwater jamboree. The fun began the night before on boats anchored off Newport and in nearby harbors. On shore the fun was more sedate, and for a time Newport almost recaptured the elegance it knew in old Cup race days when the city was the summer capital of high society and sailing was primarily a rich man's sport.

The World Cup of soccer was instituted in 1930 by the Fédération Internationale de Football (FIFA) and has been held every 4 years except when the war precluded such competition in 1942 and 1946. It has indeed grown to be one of the most popular sporting events in the world.

Life sent a team, including staff photographer Arthur Rickerby, to cover the 1966 World Cup competition in England. What they found and reported was this:

Kicking with legs that seemed made of the finest spring steel, "heading" the ball with pool-cue accuracy, and flying through the air like supermen turned Nijinskys, the world's best soccer players were squared off for the final game of the World Cup matches, one of the most exciting spectacles of sport ever witnessed. At London's Wembley Stadium, a white-shirted, precision-drilled West German team was pitted against England for the international championship of the world's most widely played and attended sport, and the honor and pride of both nations rode on every play. With 93,000 fans in the stands, Queen Elizabeth among them, another 500 million all over the world watched the spectacle on TV—including 10 million Americans, who added impetus to the already surging interest in a pro league being organized in the United States.

▼ With split-second reaction, and muscles and sinews strained to high-wire tensions, this white-shirted West German heads the ball away from his goal in the final game against England. ▶ England would not have gotten to the championship match had it not been for this header by Geoffrey Hurst, ordinarily a substitute. His header sent the ball in for the only goal of the game in the quarter-finals against Argentina.

England's players form an awesome wall to block a West German free kick in the final game. The bitterly fought, evenly matched game went to an overtime period and England finally triumphed 4–2. Three of the Britishers' four goals were scored by substitute Hurst. It was England's first and to this day only World Cup crown.

In pit row at the 1972 Indianapolis 500 is A. J. Foyt, labeled the "driver of the decade" in the 1960s. Foyt did not take home the Indy trophy that year but he did on four other occasions, the most of any race car driver in history.

Dr. Cary Middlecoff's expression tells the story of the 1957 U.S. Open in Toledo, Ohio. The tournament's defending champion, Middlecoff tied Dick Mayer on the last hole of the last round, only to lose in the ensuing playoff. His reaction here is to a putt that did not drop.

▲ Fans filled perhaps the most lopsided, cavernous baseball stadium ever for the 1959 World Series in Los Angeles. The Coliseum, an amphitheater much more attuned to football games, Olympic extravaganzas, and other assorted pageants, was converted into a ballpark by the Dodgers, who had moved to the west coast from Brooklyn the year before. While the center field wall was a distant but respectable 440 feet from home plate, the left field foul line stretched a mere 251 feet. But it could accommodate enormous crowds. More than 92,000 fans filled it for each of the three games the Dodgers hosted the Chicago White Sox that Series, dwarfing the players and the game itself, and setting single-game attendance figures that still stand. ▼ In a crucial misplay in the eighth inning of the second game of the 1959 World Series, Sherm Lollar of the White Sox is out by a proverbial mile, trying to score from first on a double by Al Smith with what would have been the game-tying run. Dodger catcher John Roseboro waits patiently here with the ball to tag Lollar out. The Sox lost the game and the action was described by Casey Stengel in his role as *Life* reporter: "Chicago is what you'd call stagnant."

◀ It was "body English" like this that urged and finagled Billy Casper's putts into various holes during the 1959 U.S. Open. It was a 4-footer on the fifty-fourth hole of the tournament and, according to Casper, it was important. "If I could sink that one last putt, I would go into the final 18 the next day with a comfortable three-stroke lead. If I missed it, they would have caught me." He didn't miss it, and they didn't catch him, and he took the title to America's biggest golf tournament. ▼ Defending champ Arnie Palmer had a few too many lies like the one he is blasting out of here in the 1961 Masters, and as a result had to relinquish his crown to Gary Player. Arnie regained the faith of his notorious "army" of fans the next year by earning back the Masters title.

The dominating figure in tennis in 1956 was Australian Lew Hoad, who made a run at becoming the first player since Don Budge in 1938 to score a grand slam of the four major singles championships (U.S., British, French, and Australian). He collected only three out of the four, however, falling in the U.S. championship to fellow countryman Ken Rosewall.

The majestic lure of sailing and the intensity of the race are dramatically portrayed in George Silk's evocative photo of sailing men in action aboard *Constellation* during the 1964 America's Cup trials. As *Life* observed, "Secrets of command—anticipation, intuition, feel of a going boat—come together in *Constellation's* afterguard: navigator Rod Stephens *(left)*, helmsman Bob Bavier, skipper Eric Ridder." *Constellation* won the trials and subsequently the coveted Cup, outrunning England's challenger *Sovereign*.

8/GAMES
SOME PEOPLE PLAY

◄ Polo, the sport of the very rich, whose rosters commonly carried uncommon names like Whitney and Vanderbilt, whose sprawling, grassy fields were often out back on someone's estate, went indoors just after World War II. Played on a compressed field in an armory like this one on Manhattan's east side, the action was fast, furious, and the spills were frequent and bone-rattling. Gjon Mili, with his high-speed lighting equipment, froze this moment—the ball just hit, the horses at full gallop—in 1947.

It is "Eights Week" at Oxford, named for the eight-man crews who take to the waters of the Thames to race for their colleges each spring. In the background, students decked out smartly in white flannels, blazers, and boaters cheer them on from their college barges. The object of the race is to overtake and bump the boat ahead, which is what the Pembroke College eight *(foreground)* is trying to do to the Oriel eight in this 1959 race. Bumping a boat enables the bumper to move ahead of the bumped. As Eights Week progresses, the good crews and their boats move forward and the weaker ones drop astern. The boat in the lead at week's end is assured of rowing in the international Henley Regatta.

Fad of the late 1940s and 1950s, roller derby brought out the fiercest in men and women alike. *Life* referred to it as "teeth-jarring action," evidence of which is seen here as one young woman tries to slip between two others. The raucous sport of bumps and blocks, flailing elbows and knees, collisions and spills, became a top television attraction of the era, especially when the women, some of whom adopted nicknames like "Toughie" or "Bruises," went at it, often throwing in sideshow fights replete with hair pulling and roundhouse punches.

Pete Dawkins, Army's star halfback and Heisman Trophy winner the year before, runs with the ball in a football game of another sort in 1959. While at Oxford on a Rhodes scholarship, the autumnal urge to carry a pigskin was apparently too compelling, and with the fall of the first few leaves he was on the rugby field. He showed some of his American football skills here, but he was informed after the run that in English football it would have been better to pass the ball or kick it. After the game he was philosophical about it, as only an Oxonian should be: "I did all sorts of things that just aren't done," Dawkins said. "But after all I didn't come to Oxford just to play football."

The bloodiest and cruelest of all sports spectacles is cockfighting, which even when this picture was taken in 1939 was illegal practically everywhere. Gjon Mili went to a clandestine fight staged in the hills about 50 miles outside New York City to photograph the fury and the gore of the fight while spectators wagered on the gruesome outcome. In this particular photo, shot at 1/100,000 of a second, the cocks, with sharp steel gaffs tied over their sawed-off spurs, are thrust at each other to get them mad at the start of the fight. As one "cocker" (the owner and trainer of a fighting cock) told Mili afterwards, "A good cock is mean, proud and beautiful. He is a sex maniac and hates every other cock. He will fight as long as he can move the steel gaffs which his owner ties to his shanks to increase his destructive power. He will fight even when his lung is punctured and a bloody rattle comes from his throat. Then he will die."

▲ The game called hurling is the national pastime of Ireland. Played with sticks called hurleys, the sport is a kind of cross between field hockey and lacrosse and can be as fast-moving and rough as both those sports. Here Father Cuchulain Moriarity, team chaplain, tosses the ball between his legs to start the action at a practice session, then will hustle to the sideline to avoid the melee which is sure to ensue.

◀ *Life* went to an imperial duck hunt at Japanese emperor Hirohito's private preserve outside Tokyo in 1946. The sport, certainly different from the occidental version, has a set of rules which were explained by the Emperor's Grand Master of the Hunt, and reported by *Life*:

The rules were ingenious, if not entirely fair to the ducks. Each hunter was equipped with a large but light and very maneuverable net on the end of a bamboo pole. He then concealed himself with nine other hunters behind a high duck blind. On the other side of the blind was a narrow canal in which were swimming wild ducks lured there by live decoys. At a signal from a gamekeeper, the sportsmen ran out quietly from behind the blind and stood along the banks of the canal, virtually on top of their game. As the frightened ducks flew up into the air, the high point of the hunt was reached. In a welter of swishing nets and clattering bamboo handles, the hunters swung their nets at the almost helpless birds. Everybody caught at least one duck.

But the lucky duck in this photo got away.

▶ Pro soccer came to the United States in 1967; it featured raucous excitement and sometimes novel encounters on the field, such as this one between a St. Louis Star (9) and a California Clipper. Most of the players in the new American soccer league were imported (the Star here is from Poland and the Clipper from Costa Rica), and few of the curious spectators understood what was taking place on the field, at least when the sport was in its infancy in the United States.

▲ To some it would seem a hobby, to others maybe a behavioral eccentricity, but to these top spinners of 1945 it was a true sport, one to challenge the limits of any man's dexterity. These middle-aged athletes developed their special form of top spinning as youngsters on the streets of Chicago, called it the "jerk system," in which they eschewed the ground for the hand. After attaining a certain level of proficiency, they could keep their tops spinning almost indefinitely, which opened the door to the invention of a wide-ranging array of maneuvers, such as the one illustrated here called "Come to Daddy." *Life* noted that, if nothing else, it was an inexpensive sport, what with tops selling for 4 cents in 1945 and the string another penny.

▶ A novel way to fish: no pole, no line, no bait, no lures. Just a crew of cormorants. The fisherman from Tungchow, near Peking, China is about to embark on just such a fishing excursion in 1946. The cormorants, diving birds, are trained to roost on the boat until thrown overboard. They are tethered by grass nooses tied just loose enough to allow them to breathe but tight enough to prevent them from swallowing a fish. The fisherman tosses the bird into the air, it circles, and when it spots a fish dives for it. The fisherman hauls the bird in, plucks the fish from its beak, and puts the catch on his stringer. Every so often the noose is loosened so that the cormorant can swallow a fish—to give it incentive. Cormorant fishing has been going on in China for more than 2000 years.

◄ *Life* went to the 1950 national marbles championship, held at Eaton Rapids, Michigan, to chronicle a sport where the sportsmen were kids and the requirements were concentration, precision, and the ability to thumb a marble in a very straight line. Here the soon-to-be winner eyes one of the seven marbles he must knock out of a 10-foot clay-surfaced ring and knuckles down for the shot. He is Tilton Holt, 12 years old, of Wilmington, Delaware, who went by the nickname ''Pork Chop'' and had to beat out 40 other city and state champs for the title of national champion.

▼ The state of the art in sport at Eton is cricket, the game so earnestly in play here on the school grounds in 1938. Generally considered to be England's national summer pastime, cricket's origin can be traced back to the thirteenth century.

Archers the world over, it seems, are as concerned with their outfits as they are about where their arrows go. A regal member of the Woodmen of Arden, a society of British archers, following the flight of his arrow here during the Grand Wardmote, their most important tourney each year, is garbed in the traditional green tailcoat, white trousers, and hat "of one's choosing." The archers of Arden also have a quaint custom: when an especially good shot is made the archer lies on his back on the ground and kicks his feet in the air, a signal for a decanter of port to be rushed onto the field for toasts.

Less traditional in the United States, costuming at archery meets is unrestricted and can range from ordinary T-shirts to slightly more elaborate outfits. The contestant at the 1962 National Archery Tournament in Las Vegas, fetching an arrow from his quiver, came clad in the attire of his favorite bowman, Robin Hood.

Lacrosse: the Cherokees called it "the little brother of death."

Life described it this way:

The webbed sticks flail like war clubs. Padded elbows smash against leather helmets and unpadded midsections. With all the elegant savagery of an Indian war dance, another lacrosse season begins. Long America's oldest contact sport—it dates back to an Indian contest called baggataway—lacrosse now has become its fastest growing sport. Lacrosse requires less brawn than other sports such as football, but it demands quickness and, above all, the desire for combat that the American Indians brought to it. Though some tribes regarded it as a religious rite to heal the sick, most used it to train young warriors for combat.

The first lacrosse game of record in American history occurred on June 4, 1763 at Fort Michilimackinac, Michigan. The Chippewa and Sac Indians arranged the game ostensibly to honor King George III. The British were so flattered many came out to watch. When the ball flew over the wall, the gate was opened to retrieve it. The Indians then grabbed their tomahawks and proceeded to butcher the garrison.

It is violent in its own way today. These photographs, taken by Arthur Rickerby at a game between Army and Navy in 1969, capture the thunder of the brutal game it is.

◀ Going for the ball, which can only be moved by stickwork, a Navy man overshoots it and an Army player is ready to pounce on it.

▶ An Army attackman drives through two Navy defenders but not, as they say, unmolested.

◀ The decidedly physical nature of the game is fairly evident in the bruising block an Army man lays on his Navy opponent.

▶ A jump for joy—Army's No. 5 has just scored a goal.

9/BASKETBALL

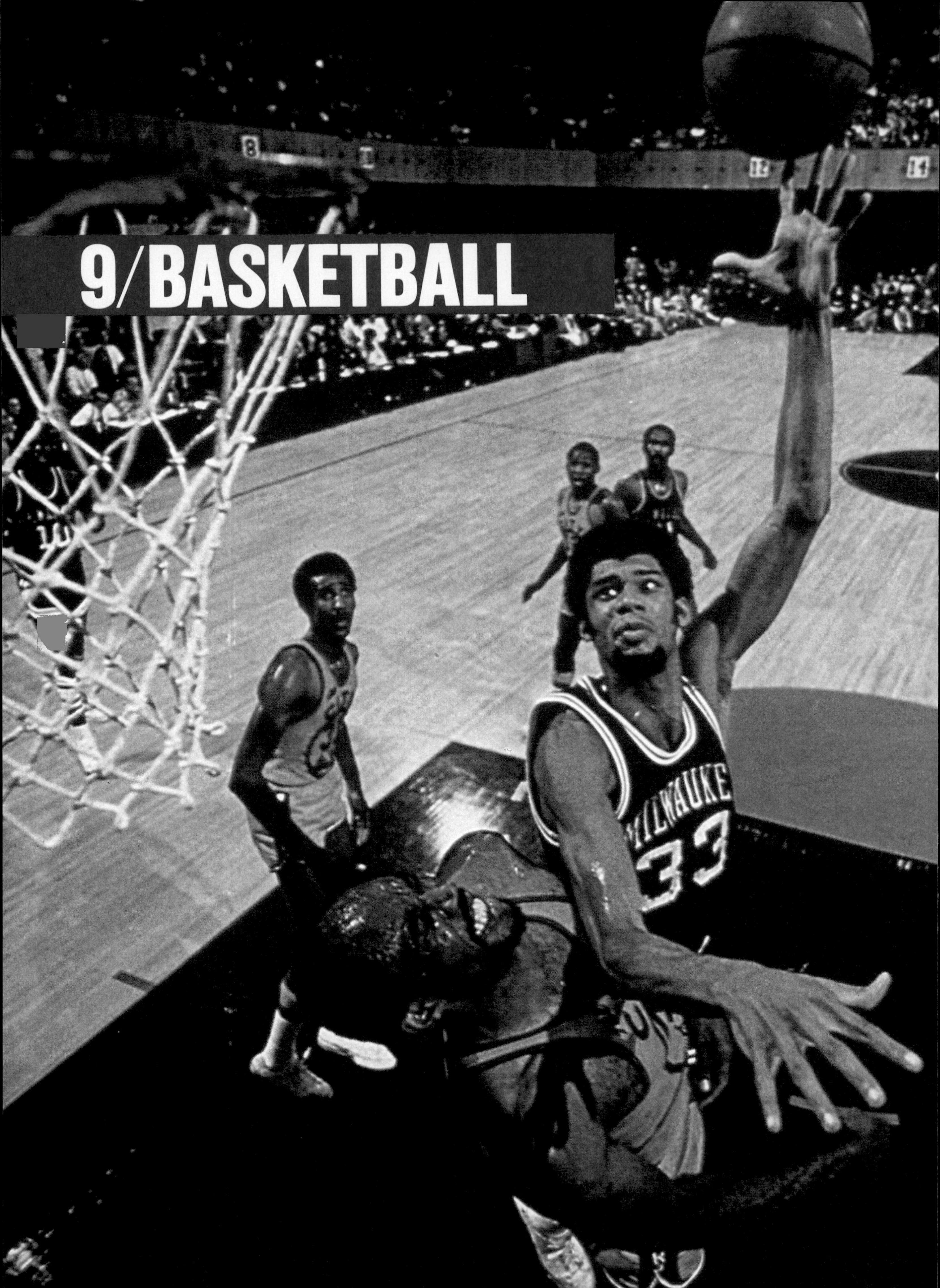

Basketball was clearly a different game in 1940 when *Life* touted Ralph Lincoln Vaughn of Southern California, dropping in a lefthanded lay-up here, as the best college hoopster in the nation. It was the age when the playmaking, set-shot-shooting guard controlled the game, free throws were often shot underhand, the jump shot was a rarity, and absolutely no one slam-dunked a ball.

◀ By 1969 Lew Alcindor had changed his name to Kareem Abdul-Jabbar and traded his UCLA uniform for that of the Milwaukee Bucks. Just how dominating he was in his first year in the NBA is clear here as he overwhelms San Francisco Warrior Nate Thurmond and loops in a hook. Named Rookie of the Year, Jabbar was so good one writer suggested the award be retitled "Best Rookie Ever." He later moved to the Los Angeles Lakers, where he remained the game's premier center through the 1970s. By the 1980s, he had become the top scorer in NBA history.

The first of the 7-footers to make a mark on the basketball court, Bob Kurland of the Oklahoma A&M Aggies, introduced the dunk. He brought his legendary coach Hank Iba two NCAA championships in 1945 and 1946 and was named the tourney's outstanding player each year.

Action here is supplied by the best college basketball team of the late 1940s, Adolph Rupp's Kentucky five. Cliff Barker drives for two in this photo while All-American guard Ralph Beard watches. Along with other All-Americans like Alex Groza and Wah Wah Jones, Kentucky won the NIT in 1946 and the NCAA championships in 1948 and 1949.

▲ "Easy Ed" Macauley, one of college basketball's finest centers in 1949, lofts one of his patented lefthanded hooks against Southern Methodist. The agile 6-foot 8-inch pivot man led St. Louis U. to the 1948 NIT championship and was named the tourney's MVP.

▼ The only team ever to win both the NCAA and NIT championships in the same year, the CCNY cagers of 1950. Seated from the left: Ed Warner, Irwin Dambrot, Ed Roman, Floyd Lane; standing: assistant coach Bobby Sand, Alvin Roth, Norm Mager, coach Nat Holman. A year later, revelations of shaving points and bribes from gamblers, as well as recruiting and scholastic violations, terminated and tarnished CCNY's double-starred achievement.

"Basketball in the borscht belt," it was called, but actually it was the best of college basketball players getting together in 1950 at a resort area in New York's Catskill Mountains. As *Life* reported, "They go there through no great love of the thick beet soup for which the region is named; rather they go because basketball is the Catskills' most popular form of entertainment. Forty borscht belt hotels have teams. Rivalry is sharp, and hotel owners offer players jobs as waiters, bellhops, and lifeguards with the understanding that they will also play basketball (two nights a week)." Here, in the shadow of the Ambassador Hotel, Bradley's Ed Behnke comes around for a reverse lay-up. At far left is North Carolina State's All-American Dick Dickey.

◀ Driving for a lay-up is Duke's one-man scoring machine, Dick Groat, in a 1951 encounter with Temple. A 6-foot guard, Groat set a national collegiate scoring record the year before when he amassed 831 points for Duke. After college, Groat chose major league baseball as his profession and had a fine career as shortstop for the Pittsburgh Pirates and the St. Louis Cardinals.

▶ The team to watch in 1950 was the St. Johns Redmen, then located in Brooklyn, giant killers by their own definition. In the process of defeating San Francisco, the previous year's NIT champs, center Bob Zawoluk (27) battles for a rebound while guard Al McGuire (18), later to inscribe his name in basketball lore as a coach and TV commentator, looks on. Earlier in the season, the Redmen knocked off NCAA defending champs, Kentucky.

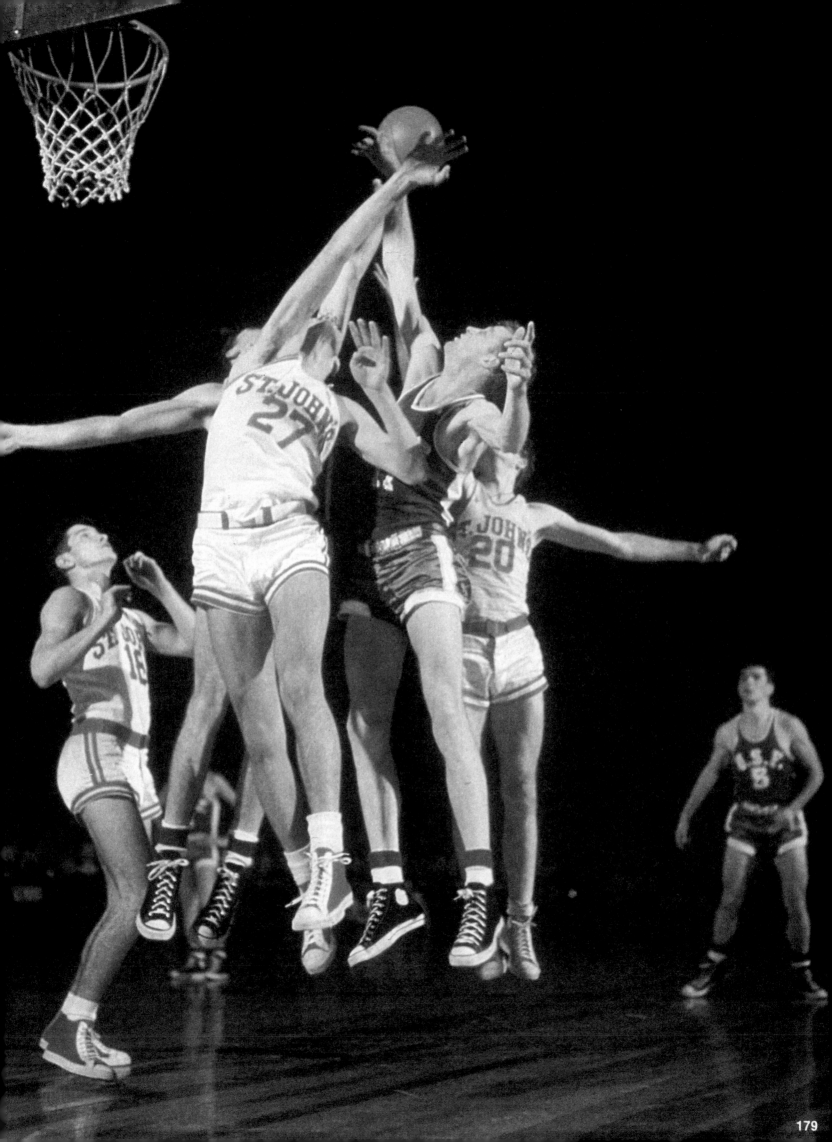

◄ The incomparable Reece "Goose" Tatum goes into his act for the Harlem Globetrotters. Called "basketball's court jester," Tatum and his colleagues put on their zany acts on the court throughout the United States and overseas everywhere from Berlin to Malaya.

▼ Even triple teaming, as Presbyterian College is doing here, could not stop Furman's voracious scorer Frank Selvy. Shooting left-handed and right-handed, Selvy racked up 48 points in this 1954 contest. The 100 points he scored against Newbury stands as the most ever scored in a single college game.

◀ The young man who brought the NCAA crown to LaSalle College of Philadelphia in 1954, Tom Gola makes it look easy here against Penn Military College. Gola was a consensus All-American and received the NCAA's outstanding player award.

▼ Oscar Robertson was a 19-year-old sophomore when this photo was taken, and already an uncontested All-American selection. The "Big O" starred for the University of Cincinnati from 1958 through 1960, and when he graduated he had accumulated more points than any player in college basketball history. He went on to have a spectacular pro career with the Cincinnati Royals and the Milwaukee Bucks, and when he retired, he held the all-time NBA records for most assists and most free throws made, and only a handful of players have scored more than O's 26,710 career points (an average of 25.7 a game).

▲ A pure pro at work, Bob Pettit grabs a rebound for his St. Louis Hawks in a 1959 contest with the New York Knicks. A two-time NBA MVP, and selected to the first team of the NBA All-Star team 10 years in a row, Pettit was inducted into the Basketball Hall of Fame in 1970. ◄ The best in the west in 1958 was Seattle's Elgin Baylor, dropping in an easy one here. Baylor did everything for Seattle, leading the team in scoring and rebounding, serving as playmaker and floor captain, and taking his small college all the way to the NCAA championship game. They lost there to Kentucky, but Baylor was honored as the tournament's MVP.

▶Bob Cousy could handle a basketball with consummate skill, mystifying opponents and bedazzling spectators with his dribbling and passing. Besides that he was an artful shooter. Long the captain of the Celtics, he led them to five NBA titles and was named to the pro's first-team All-Stars ten times. Here he drives through Jim Paxson (11) and Bob Leonard of the Minneapolis Lakers in 1960. His coach, Red Auerbach, was delighted to find how wrong he was when he said after Cousy arrived to try out for the Celtics in 1950: "We need a big man. Little men are a dime a dozen."

◀Battle of the titans or collision of the giants, those were the kinds of terms used to describe the intense and brutal confrontations of 7-foot 2-inch Wilt Chamberlain, the game's most profuse scorer, and 6-foot 11-inch Bill Russell, basketball's greatest defensive center, when they met on the pro circuit in the 1960s. Philadelphia Warrior Chamberlain clearly has the controlling, if not terrorizing, hand here as he muscles a rebound far above Russell. This dramatic moment was from the 1967 NBA playoffs in which the 76ers eliminated the Celtics, a team that had won the NBA championship for 8 consecutive years.

At this time, 1967, he was known as Lew Alcindor and he was the keystone of John Wooden's invincible UCLA Bruins. During his 3 years of varsity ball, the 7-foot-plus Alcindor and his teammates won three NCAA titles and he was named the tourney's outstanding player in each. Here, he soars over Washington State's 6-foot 9-inch center Jim McKean to stuff one. Watching him is UCLA's All-American guard Mike Warren, who went on to stardom of a different sort as a cop on the television series *Hill Street Blues*.

Between the days he was setting all kinds of basketball records while playing for Princeton and those when he was sitting in a U.S. Senate seat, Bill Bradley did duty with the New York Knicks in the late 1960s and early 1970s and helped propel them to NBA championships in 1970 and 1973. Bradley, as a rookie here, was described as looking like "Henry Fonda stumbling onto the set of a basketball movie," but the Rhodes Scholar proved himself both an adept and durable pro player.

College basketball's all-time high scorer, Pete Maravich of LSU, shows off some ball-handling finesse here, dribbling through his legs without breaking stride on one of his patented drives to the basket. "Pistol Pete," as he was called, scored a total of 3667 in his three varsity seasons (1967–1970), an average of 44.2 points a game, both all-time NCAA records.

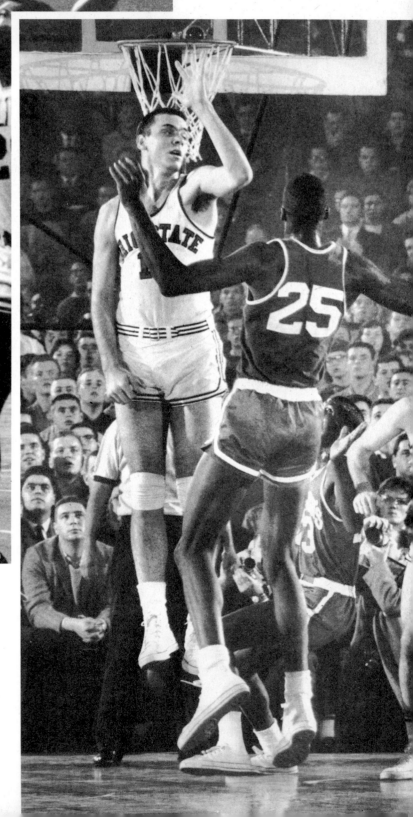

There was always a little thunder when Elvin Hayes (11) of San Diego and Kareem Abdul-Jabbar (33) battled under the boards. When the 1969–1970 season was over, Hayes, in his second year as a pro, was the leading rebounder in the NBA and third in scoring, while rookie Jabbar was second in scoring and third in rebounding.

▲ Jerry West, about to contort his way into position for a shot, displays the form and flexibility that, in 1970, enabled him to become the league's top scorer and runner-up MVP. West was elected to the NBA All-Star first team ten times, and the second team twice.

▶ Rather blasé about it is Ohio State All-American Jerry Lucas as he casually flicks away a shot by LeRoy Ellis (25) of St. Johns in a 1961 game. "Big Luke," as the 6-foot 8-inch center was known, was a big factor in the Buckeyes' successful quest for the NCAA crown the year before.

The New York Knicks won their first world championship in 1970, becoming only the second team in 12 years to lay claim to it besides the monopolistic Boston Celtics. Under coach Red Holzman, the Knicks compiled a record of 60–22 to win the NBA's eastern division.

It took the Knicks seven games to eliminate a surprising Baltimore team in the eastern semifinals, but only five to get past Kareem Abdul-Jabbar and the Milwaukee Bucks. Then in a seesaw championship series, they traded wins with the Los Angeles Lakers through six games and finally iced it on their home court in game seven.

In this essay, *Life* captured some of the playoff's fierce action, and zeroed in on three of the Knicks who were key contributors to the New Yorkers' good fortune.

▼ The Knicks ballhandler was Walt Frazier, whose 629 assists was the second best in the NBA that year. Frazier also averaged 20.9 points per game, ran fourth in the MVP voting, and was a first-team All-Star.

▶ Willis Reed, a good 5 inches shorter than defender Kareem Abdul-Jabbar, drives around him for two in the eastern finals. Reed led the Knicks in scoring that year with 1755 points (21.7 average), and in rebounding (1126) and was named the NBA's Most Valuable Player. ▼ Driving here is Dave DeBusschere, acknowledged as one of the game's all-time great defensive players. He also averaged 14.6 points a game during the regular season.

10/PORTRAITS

◄Cal Hubbard, the only man elected to both the Pro Football Hall of Fame (for his play with the New York Giants and the Green Bay Packers) and the Baseball Hall of Fame (as an umpire). As a Giant in 1936 here, he was earning about a $150 a game.

◄Jimmy Demaret, golf's most fanciful fashion plate, and a leading member of the circuit in the 1940s and 1950s, winner of the Masters twice.

▲ Joe Louis, in training for his 1948 fight with Jersey Joe Walcott, the Brown Bomber's twenty-fifth title defense. He wore the heavyweight crown from 1937 through 1948.

◄Frankie Frisch, relaxing in his last year with the St. Louis Cardinals, was honorary chairman of the board of the Cards' Gas House Gang from 1927 through 1937 after having played 8 years with the New York Giants. He later managed the Cardinals, Pirates, and Cubs.

Yogi Berra, at age 24, as he appeared for the New York Yankees in 1949, early in his career. Yogi caught for the Yanks for 18 years and later managed the team on two different occasions.

Manolete, the world's *numero uno* matador in the 1940s. Born Manuel Rodriguez, at age 30 in 1947 he was gored to death after having earned more than $4 million in the *corrida*.

Marcel Cerdan, training for his upcoming title bout with Tony Zale in 1948. The Frenchman held the world middleweight title in 1948 and 1949.

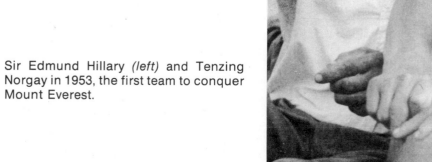

Sir Edmund Hillary *(left)* and Tenzing Norgay in 1953, the first team to conquer Mount Everest.

◀ Jackie Robinson, weary and dejected in the autumn of his career. He played for Brooklyn from 1947 through 1956, batting a career .311.

A recently retired Rosey Grier, doing needlepoint. When he wasn't at his hobby, he was one of the most fearsome defensive lineman ever to wear a New York Giant uniform in the late 1950s and early 1960s.

▲ Gussie Moran, appropriately nick-named "Gorgeous" and later involved in the lace panties controversy, looks de-mure in 1949 photo.

▲ Above: Varipapa shown in 1949 bowl championship.

NO.	NAME	GAMES	WON	LOST	PINS	POINTS	EX. PT.
1	A. VARIPAPA	64	40½	23½	13448	309-23	
2	J. WILMAN	64	40½	23½	13431	309-06	
3	S. SLOMENSKI	64	38	26	13123	301-23	○
4	S. NAGY	64	32	32	13250	297-00	
5	B. BOMAR	64	31	33	13188	295-38	○
6	W. WARD	64	34	30	12842	290-42	
7	T. SPARANDO	64	32	32	12887	290-37	○
8	C. JOHNSON Jr.	64	33½	30½	12820	289-45	
9	E. BOTTEN	64	35	29	12724	289-24	
10	C. O'DONNELL	64	34	30	12544	284-44	
11	B. KENET	64	33	31	12584	284-34	
12	L. ROLLICK	64	29	35	12746	283-46	
13	W. JOHNSON	64	25	39	12560	277-10	○
14	F. HAYNES	64	29½	34½	12377	277-02	
15	D. COMINS	64	27	37	12434	275-34	
16	F. CLAUSE	64	18	46	12222	262-22	
17	J. ZACK	ALTERNATE					

OFFICIAL STANDING
ALL STAR TOURNAMENT

J. WILMAN	36	7821
A. VARIPAPA	36	7478

Ernest Hemingway and Antonio Ordóñez, aficionado and premier matador, at ringside in Spain in 1960.

Emil Zatopek, the greatest long distance runner since Paavo Nurmi. The Czech won three Olympic gold medals in 1952, when this portrait was taken, triumphing in the 5000- and 10,000-meter runs and the marathon.

Sugar Ray Robinson in a pensive moment before the 35-year-old boxer would enter the ring in 1955 to try to regain the middleweight crown from Bobo Olson. Sugar Ray held the world welterweight title for 5 years and the middleweight title over a span of 7 years, and won 175 of his 202 professional fights.

Citation, after having just set two world's records in 1948: running the mile in 1 minute, 33.6 seconds and amassing a career money-winning total of $924,630. "Big Cy" also won the Triple Crown that year.

Rocky Marciano, pondering his pending 1952 title fight with Jersey Joe Walcott. The only heavyweight champ to retire undefeated (49 victories, 45 by knockout), he held the title from 1952 to 1956.

Grantland Rice *(right),* legendary sports scrivener, and Bernie Bierman, University of Minnesota coach, talking football over lunch at Toots Shor's. The topic was unlimited substitution, which was a new and controversial rule in 1948.

▶ Sal Maglie, intent, baleful, and 39 years old, now a Brooklyn Dodger, the team he so often subdued in seven earlier seasons as a New York Giant. With 13 wins, he helped the Dodgers to the 1956 pennant, and shortly after he retired with 119 career victories and an impressive won-lost percentage of .657.

▼ Kid Gavilan, sweat-beaded and bedraggled after losing a middleweight title fight to Bobo Olson in 1954. Gavilan had claim to the welterweight title from 1951 to 1954.

▶ Vince Lombardi, fierce-eyed, miracle-making coach of the Green Bay Packers. A former member of Fordham's ''seven blocks of granite,'' Lombardi took over a last-place Packer team in 1959 and turned it into a dynasty, winning five NFL titles and compiling a record of 89-24-4.

Silky Sullivan, hamming it up before the Kentucky Derby in 1958. Famous for his come-from-far-behind finishes, he forgot about his reputation Derby Day and came in twelfth while Tim Tam took the classic.

Arnie Palmer, the first golfer to exceed $1 million in earnings. Palmer won the Masters four times, the British Open twice, the U.S. Open, and the U.S. Amateur.

Jim Brown, brooding Cleveland Brown, the greatest running back of his generation. When he retired in 1965, he had rushed for the most yards (12,312), scored the most touchdowns (106), and had the best average gain (5.22 yards) in the history of pro football.

▶ Walt Alston (left) and Leo Durocher, with matching crow's feet and Los Angeles Dodger uniforms, watch the spring training workouts at Dodgertown in Vero Beach, Florida, in 1964.

Gary Player, undaunted and undampened in winning the 1965 Masters. The South African also collected first prizes in the U.S. Open and British Open and as a PGA champ.

El Cordobés, out of his matador's finery. Born Manuel Benitez, he was Spain's most unorthodox yet most popular bullfighter of the late 1960s and early 1970s.

Carl Yastrzemski. Not since Ted Williams was there such a Boston Red Sox legend. From 1961 into the 1980s he roamed the outfield at Fenway Park and ended his 23-year career at age 44 in 1983 assured of a first-class ticket to the Baseball Hall of Fame.

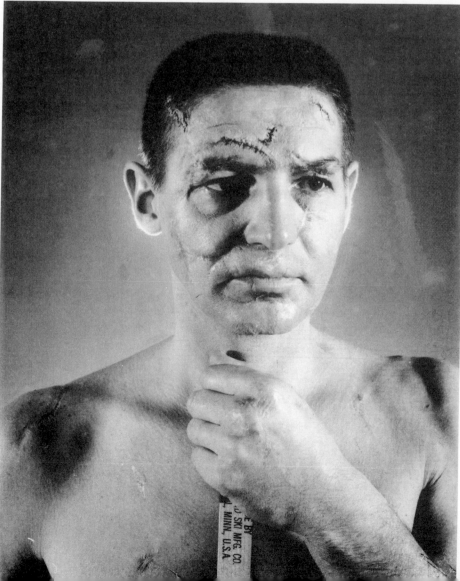

Terry Sawchuk, Toronto Maple Leaf goalie, wears the marks of his trade. Actually the scars were recreated by a make-up man to show the more than 400 stitches sewn in Sawchuk's face in 16 years of goal tending.

Jean Claude Killy on the Swiss slopes, 23 years old in 1967, was justly heralded as the world's greatest racing skier. At the 1968 winter Olympics the Frenchman captured gold medals in three events: downhill racing, slalom, and giant slalom. Killy was also the winner of the first two Alpine World Cup competitions.

Jack Nicklaus, destined to become the world's wealthiest athlete, is captured in portrait here, doing what he did so often, dropping a crucial putt. This was at the playoff with Arnie Palmer at the National Open in Pittsburgh in 1962, which Nicklaus won. Over the years, Nicklaus won five Masters tournaments; five PGA titles, four U.S. Opens, and three British Opens.

Charley Finley, controversial owner of the Oakland A's, cooling off. Described as headstrong, mercurial, sensitive to criticism, and given to bizarre gestures, he still brought Oakland world championships in 1972, 1973, and 1974.

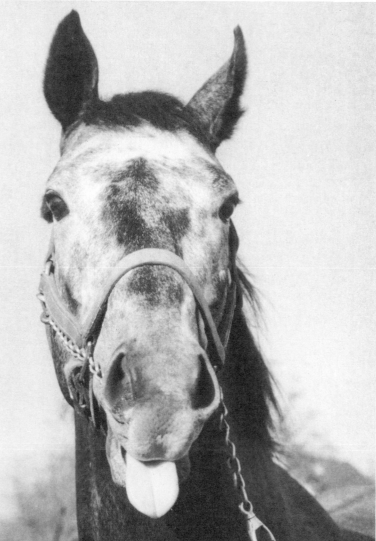

Dancer's Image, disdaining the camera with his own brand of raspberries. He had finished first in the 1968 Kentucky Derby but was disqualified after traces of a drug were found in his system; he was forced to turn over the prize money and victor's blanket of roses to runner-up Forward Pass.

▲ The craggy face of Casey Stengel, a man who saw baseball from the field and the dugout for 57 years. Coming up as a player in 1912, he batted .284 over 14 years; managing, the "Old Perfesser" brought ten pennants home for the Yankees.

◀ Lee Trevino, with characteristic cool, doffs his golfing shoes and waits out a summer downpour in 1971. Winner of the U.S. Open, the PGA, and two British Opens, he was also known as the "mad golfer" for his antic behavior on the links.

▲ Gil Hodges, saddened and troubled at times by his New York Mets, the perennial cellar dwellers, of the National League East, brought them out of the doldrums and to a world championship in 1969, the year this picture was snapped.

◀ Mario Andretti, the stress of high-speed auto racing etched forever in his face. He won the Indy 500 in 1969 and was a three-time U.S. Auto Club national champ.

Muhammad Ali uncharacteristically gagged here in 1963. "The Greatest," a 1960 Olympic gold medalist, is the only boxer in history to win the heavyweight title three times.

▲ Joe Frazier, somber champion, awaiting the ultimate challenge from Muhammad Ali in 1971.

▶ Woody Hayes, swelled to the occasion, watches over his Ohio State Buckeyes in the 1960s. The often controversial Hayes won 238 games during his 33 years of coaching at Denison, Miami (Ohio), and OSU.

During the 1960 summer Olympics in Rome this was a monumental and certainly appropriate setting for the Greco-Roman wrestling matches—the ruins of the Basilica of Maxentius near the Colosseum.

The 1948 winter Olympic Games were held in the picturesque Alps of St. Moritz, Switzerland, and the summer games convened in London. In this first postwar Olympiad Germany and Japan were conspicuously absent, and the United States dominated just about everything in swimming and men's track and field except for the distance races.

The two most noteworthy performances at the summer games were turned in by 17-year-old Bob Mathias of California, who won the decathlon, and the Netherlands' Fanny Blankers-Koen, who won gold medals in the women's 100- and 200-meter dashes and the 80-meter hurdles.

Other winners of note included sprinters Harrison Dillard (100 meters) and Mel Patton (200 meters), Mal Whitfield in the 800-meter run, hurdlers Bill Porter (110 meters) and Roy Cochran (400 meters), Emil Zatopek of Czechoslovakia in the 10,000-meter run, and Belgium's Gaston Reiff in the 5000-meter race.

In the winter games, it was Canada's Barbara Ann Scott dominating women's figure skating and Dick Button of the United States in the men's event.

▲ Emil Zatopek, anguished and strained, moves out in the last lap of the 10,000-meter run. He finished in 29 minutes, 59.6 seconds, an Olympic record.

High-flying Dick Button executes a perfect split jump in the shadow of the Swiss Alps. He racked up the highest score in Olympic figure skating up to that time.

Olympiad XV was a Scandinavian affair in 1952, the summer games in Helsinki, Finland, and the winter games at Oslo, Norway.

Czech Emil Zatopek won three gold medals, the 5000- and 10,000-meter runs and the marathon, in the latter setting an Olympic record of 2 hours, 23 minutes, 3.2 seconds. The United States won fourteen gold medals in men's track and field, with Bob Mathias and Mal Whitfield repeat winners in the decathlon and 800-meter run. Harrison Dillard went back to the hurdles and won the 110-meter race, Andy Stanfield triumphed in the 200-meter dash, and Horace Ashenfelter won the 3000-meter stee-plechase. And there was Bob Richards dominating the pole vault and Parry O'Brien the shot put.

In boxing, the gold medal in the middle-weight class went to America's Floyd Patterson, who would later put on a few pounds and take the world heavyweight title. And in the winter games, it was again Dick Button who was matchless in figure skating.

▼ A broken-hearted broad jumper, George Brown of UCLA, the Olympic favorite, was disqualified after fouling for the third time on his final leaps.

◀ With perfect form, U.S. diver Pat McCormick heads for the water. She won both the high-dive and springboard events.

▼ A grimacing Bob Mathias completes a 22-foot, 11-inch broad jump in one of the ten events of the decathlon, in which he again earned a gold medal (the other 4 years earlier). The 21-year-old broke his own world record in the event.

Melbourne, Australia, was host to the summer Olympics in 1956, while the winter athletes met in Cortina d'Ampezzo, Italy. It was a year when Olympic track and field records fell in profusion.

One of the record-setting performers was Ron Delaney of Ireland in the 1500-meter run (3 minutes, 41.2 seconds). Record breakers from the United States included Bobby Morrow, 200-meter dash (20.6 seconds); Lee Calhoun, 110-meter hurdles (13.5 seconds); Glenn Davis, 400-meter hurdles (50.1 seconds); Bob Richards, pole vault (14 feet, 11½ inches); Charlie Dumas, high jump (6 feet, 11⁷⁄₁₆ inches); Parry O'-Brien, shot put (60 feet, 11¹⁄₁₆ inches); Al Oerter, discus (184 feet, 10⅞ inches); and Milt Campbell, decathlon (7937 points). Vladimir Kuts of the Soviet Union made his presence felt by winning both the 5000- and 10,000-meter runs. And Betty Cuthbert of Australia won three gold medals, victorious in the 100- and 200-meter dashes and as a member of the 400-meter relay team.

In diving, Pat McCormick again brought two gold medals back to the United States. Another American, Paul Anderson, was dubbed the world's strongest human after capturing the heavyweight gold in weight lifting. And a spritely Tenley Albright was the best in women's figure skating, while Russia dominated the speed skating events.

▼ A photo finish between U.S. hurdlers in a qualifying heat of the 110-meter race as Jack Davis *(left)* and Lee Calhoun hit the tape at the same time (13.8). Calhoun knocked three-tenths of a second off to win the finals and set an Olympic record.

All but one U.S. sprinter drives for the tape to qualify in the 100-meter dash. Dave Sime, one of the favorites, pulled up lame. Bobby Morrow *(right)* won the race and did the same in the Olympic finals. The others are, from the left: Willie Williams, Paul Williams, Theo Bush, Willie White, Rod Richard, and Bobby Whilden.

▲ Bobby Morrow breaks the tape to win the 200-meter dash at Melbourne. Rounding out a U.S. sweep of the event are Andy Stanfield (center), second, and Thane Baker, third.

◀ The Reverend Bob Richards sends up a sudden prayer that the teetering bar he has just vaulted over stays up. His prayer was answered, and he had a new Olympic record of 14 feet, 11½ inches.

▲ A glamorous, pensive Gunhild Larking of Sweden awaits her turn at the high jump.

◄ A prototype of power, Parry O'Brien unleashes the 16-pound shot, putting it 60 feet, 11 inches to beat the Olympic record he had set 4 years earlier.

In the classic setting of Rome, with its ancient ruins of amphitheaters and arenas, the 1960 summer games were held and new standards were set in eighteen of the twenty-four men's track and field events. The winter Olympics were hosted by the United States at Squaw Valley, California.

There were some repeat winners, athletes like Glenn Davis, Lee Calhoun, and Al Oerter, and a bevy of names new to the Olympic gold but already gemstones in the world of track and field, such as Peter Snell of New Zealand and Herb Elliott of Australia, Abebe Bikila of Ethiopia, and from the United States Rafer Johnson, Don Bragg, and Bill Nieder. In the women's competition, there was Wilma Rudolph of the United States and Tamara Press of the Soviet Union.

In boxing, there was a sensational light heavyweight champ by the name of Cassius Clay; in women's figure skating a dazzling Carol Heiss.

◄America's sensational speedster Wilma Rudolph stretches for the tape in the 100-meter dash. Crippled in childhood and unable to walk until the age of 8, Rudolph won gold medals in the 100- and 200-meter dashes and as a member of the 400-meter relay team. ▼The finish of the 100-meter dash finds a surprise winner at the tape, Armin Hary *(nearest lane)* of Germany, beating out Dave Sime *(far lane)* of the United States.

▼ The two magnificient athletes who battled so desperately for supremacy in the decathlon, C. K. Yang of Formosa and Rafer Johnson of the United States. Johnson won.

▶ An apprehensive Paula Jean Pope, favorite to win the gold medal in springboard diving, watches as her fiercest competitor, Ingrid Kramer of East Germany, completes a dive. Moments later the apprehension turned to despair as the East German diver took the gold, leaving Pope with the silver.

The first Olympic Games ever to be held in Asia were staged at Tokyo in the summer of 1964, while the winter games were held at a more traditional site, Innsbruck, Austria.

Billed as the world's fastest human, Bob Hayes of the United States won the 100-meter dash in 10 seconds flat, tying the world's record; and the world's most durable of middle-distance runners, Peter Snell of New Zealand, won both the 800- and 1500-meter runs. Abebe Bikila repeated in the marathon, so did Al Oerter in the discus (his third consecutive gold medal in the event).

The United States fielded explosive women sprinters in Wyomia Tyus and Edith McGuire and the Soviet Union collected two gold medals with Tamara Press in the women's shot put and discus throw.

Don Schollander was the top name in swimming; heavyweight Joe Frazier in boxing; and Irena Press (Tamara's sister) in a new event, the women's pentathlon.

▼ The lady loses her luge. Erica Aussendorfer of Italy sits stranded on the snow as her sled races on alone.

▲ Action like this suddenly created worldwide interest in the game of volleyball, which had never been part of Olympic competition before. The Japanese women's team, so precise and intense, astounded everyone who watched the competition. ▼ Don Schollander happily gives the victory sign after anchoring a U.S. 800-meter relay team that won the gold medal. Schollander collected four golds (two in individual freestyle sprints, two in relays), the first Olympian to earn that many since Jesse Owens did it for the United States in 1936.

A triumphant Peter Snell, after crossing the finish line in the 800-meter run. A little later he was equally successful in the 1500-meter run, becoming the first runner since 1920 to win both events in the same Olympic Games.

▶ All the emotion of ultimate victory in the Olympics is captured in this sequence as 16-year-old Cathy Ferguson stands atop platform one after winning the 100-meter backstroke, her gold medal just received and the strains of "The Star-Spangled Banner" heralding her wonderful accomplishment.

The Olympic Games moved to Latin America for the first time in the summer of 1968, being held in Mexico City, and in the high altitude of that capital a number of people jumped longer and leaped higher then humans ever had before. The winter games were staged in Grenoble, France.

The phenomenon of the games was Bob Beamon's record-shattering long jump of 29 feet, 2⅜ inches, bettering the world's record by more than 2 feet. Al Oerter once again won the discus (his fourth over 12 years). Kenya dominated the distance races, winning three gold medals: Kip Keino in the 1500-meter run, Amos Beivott in the 3000-meter steeplechase, and Nabila Temer in the 10,000-meter race.

From the United States there were outstanding performances from sprinters Jimmy Hines and Tommie Smith, hurdler Willie Davenport, and in the decathlon Bill Toomey. On the field, Bob Seagren vaulted to a record 17 feet, 5⅝ inches, Dick Fosbury "Fosbury-flopped" 7 feet, 4³⁄₁₆ inches, and Randy Matson heaved the shot 67 feet, 4¹¹⁄₁₆ inches. Wyomia Tyus repeated in the women's 100-meter dash.

U.S. swimmers collected a pot of gold in men's competition with the likes of Mike Barton and Charles Hickox, and in the women's events with Debbie Meyer and Claudia Kolb. In boxing, there was heavyweight champ George Foreman.

At the winter Olympics the incomparable Frenchman Jean Claude Killy dominated the skiing events, and in figure skating it was the ethereal Peggy Fleming.

▶ Bob Seagren soars over the bar for the United States, vaulting to a gold medal and a new Olympic record (17 feet, 5⅝ inches).

A moment of protest in keeping with an age of controversy came about when Tommie Smith (center) winner of the 200-meter dash and teammate John Carlos raised gloved hands during the playing of the U.S. national anthem. Their purpose was to publicize and protest against alleged discrimination against blacks in sports and other fields of endeavor in the United States.

The 1972 summer Olympic Games in Munich were forever scarred by the invasion of terrorists and the killing of ten Israeli athletes and a coach. The winter games were conducted in Sapporo, Japan.

Mark Spitz of the United States turned in the most sensational performance that year, winning seven gold medals in swimming competition. Roland Matthes of East Germany, another superb swimmer, repeated wins from the previous Olympiad in the 100- and 200-meter backstroke races. In women's swimming, Shane Gould of Australia went home with three gold medals.

The U.S. predominance in track and field was not in evidence at Olympiad XX. U.S.S.R. sprinter Valery Borzov won both the 100- and 200-meter dashes, and Lasse Viren of Finland captured first place in the 5000- and 10,000-meter runs. But a few Americans earned the gold: Frank Shorter in the marathon, Dave Wottle in the 800-meter run, and Rod Milburn in the 110-meter hurdles, while Randy Williams took the long jump. In women's track and field, the U.S. did not take a single gold medal.

In boxing, Teofilo Stevenson of Cuba barely worked up a sweat to win the heavyweight division. And Olga Korbut made her debut in women's gymnastics.

▼ A grand opening to the winter games at Sapporo, Japan.

◀ 18-year-old Janet Lynn of the United States, smiling even in the face of adversity, won a bronze medal in women's figure skating.

▼ Rod Milburn *(fourth from the left)* of the United States leads in the 110-meter hurdles, an event he won, and in so doing he tied the world's record of 13.2 seconds.

Two American winners: with his lucky teddy bear, Randy Williams, long jumper; wearing his good-luck hat, Dave Wottle, tops in the 800-meter run.

◄ A tearful Olga Korbut of Russia learns that she has not won the all-around title in gymnastics. But the next night, the 4-foot 11-inch 84-pound 17-year-old gathered golds in beam exercises and free exercises.

◀ The ecstasy of triumph explodes from East Germany's Wolfgang Nordwig as he clears 18 feet, ½ inch to capture the gold medal in the pole vault.

▶ "The fastest swimmer ever" he was billed, and Mark Spitz of the United States, holder at the time of twenty-four world records, lived up to his reputation by winning an unprecedented seven gold medals.

▶ A jubilant U.S. basketball team celebrates the winning of an Olympic championship, defeating the Soviet Union in the last 3 seconds of the game, 50–49. But it was premature because the top official ordered 3 seconds put back on the clock and the Russians threw a full-court pass to a player who, heavily guarded, somehow grabbed it and dropped it in to reverse the outcome.

There were 16,000 soldiers and policemen on hand to protect the 6000 athletes at the 1976 summer Olympic Games in Montreal, Canada, with memories of the tragedy of four years earlier too terribly fresh. But the Olympiad was unmarred and became a showcase of majestic talent.

The most dazzling was 14-year-old Nadia Comenici of Rumania, who with almost supernatural grace won 3 gold medals in gymnastics as well as a silver and a bronze. Equally sublime, but on a floor of ice, was America's Dorothy Hamill.

The Soviet Union captured 47 gold medals. East Germany 40, and the United States 34 during the summer games. There were edifying performances everywhere. Alberto Juantorena of Cuba won both the 400- and 800-meter runs. Lasse Viren of Sweden repeated a victory in the 10,000-meter race. A blithe Edwin Moses of the United States triumphed in the 400-meter hurdles and Bruce Jenner brought the decathlon gold back to the United States.

Women's track and field and swimming were dominated by the East Germans, and men's swimming by the United States. In boxing there was Sugar Ray Leonard and the Spinks brothers, Michael and Leon, from the United States, and heavyweight Teofilo Stevenson of Cuba.

In the 1980 winter Olympics at Lake Placid, New York, there was the overwhelming presence of Eric Heiden who swept the speed skating gold medals, and the amazing American hockey team that surprised the world.

The following summer, for the first time in the history of the modern Olympic Games, the United States did not attend the summer games, which were held in Moscow. Track and field and swimming medals were heavily dominated by the Russians and the East Germans as a result.

There were memorable performances from Sebastian Coe of England in the 1500-meter race, Miruts Yifter of Ethiopia who won both the 5000- and 10,000-meter runs, Walter Cierpinski of East Germany who repeated a gold medal in the marathon, a world record breaking pole vault of 18 feet 11½ inches by Wladyslaw Kozakiewicz of Poland, and the athletic magnificence of Daley Thompson of England in the decathlon.

▶ Eric Heiden worked hard before the 1980 Olympic Games, and part of his training was this: speed skating on roller skates during the iceless months. The special skates substituting for speed-skate blades were, ironically, developed by the Russians for their aspirants to the Olympic gold. Heiden here uses them on a Wisconsin road. And they must have helped because he won gold medals at Lake Placid in the 500-, 1000-, 1500-, 5000-, and 10,000-meter speed skating races, something that had never before been accomplished at an Olympiad.

◀ The United States hockey team in the ecstasy of victory, and an unexpected triumph at that. The heavily favored U.S.S.R. icemen fell to the Americans, jubilation prevailed, and the United States had its first set of gold medals in hockey since 1960.

In the 1984 winter games, held in Sarajevo, Yugoslavia, Scott Hamilton became the first U.S. male figure skater to win the gold since 1960. Phil Mahr became the first American ever to win the gold in the slalom, while Bill Johnson duplicated this achievement in the downhill. Debbie Armstrong won the giant slalom in the women's competition.

It was the Soviet Union who declined to attend the summer 1984 games in Los Angeles. As a result, the United States won an unprecedented 83 gold medals.

There were superb performances at every level. Speedster Carl Lewis of the United States won both the 100- and 200-meter dashes, Sebastian Coe of England repeated a gold in the 1500-meter run, Edwin Moses again triumphed in the 400-meter hurdles after an 8-year interlude, and the U.S. 400-meter relay team set a new world record.

On the inner fields, Carl Lewis captured another gold in the long jump. And Daley Thompson of England won the decathlon, scoring more points with his 8797 than any human ever had before in the Olympics.

Among the women, Valerie Brisco-Hooks of the United States won both the 200- and 400-meter races, and Joan Benoit, another American, became the first to win the newly instituted women's marathon. And, of course, Mary Decker fell and Zola Budd was injured in the 3000-meter run, neither finishing in the precious metal.

The United States monopolized the medals in swimming. Greg Louganis took golds in both springboard and platform diving, and in women's swimming Tiffany Cohen (400 and 800 meters), Mary Meagher (100- and 200-meter butterfly), and Tracy Caulkins (200- and 400-meter individual medley) were double gold winners. And in gymnastics, there was the enrapturing Mary Lou Retton of the United States.

A collision, then anguish. It was the Olympics' most searing image: a face contorted with rage and pain and despair. Favored to win the 3000 meters, Mary Decker, 26, was leading when Zola Budd, the barefoot South African running for Great Britain, passed her close on the outside. Decker tripped and went down in an agony that was more than physical.

◀ The ultimate moment of triumph. Carl Lewis leaps in exaltation as he carries the baton across the tape to win the 400-meter relay. In doing so, Lewis and his running mates set a new world record of 37.83 seconds. Lewis won three other gold medals in the 1984 Olympics, but to him, "The most exciting is the relay—you have three other runners to worry about. Will they stumble? Will they drop the baton?" Needless to say, they didn't.

▲ A handspring into the record books. As an American moment it was a perfect 10. The move was a layout back somersault with a double twist, and in order to beat her nearest rival in the women's all-around gymnastic championship, Mary Lou Retton needed a flawless score. Spangled in stars and stripes, her sinewy 92 pounds gyrated through space as if she had repealed the law of gravity. It was the first individual Olympic medal in gymnastics ever won by an American woman. Recalls 16-year-old Retton, who wound up with one gold, two silvers, and two bronzes, "I had goose bumps going up and down me!"

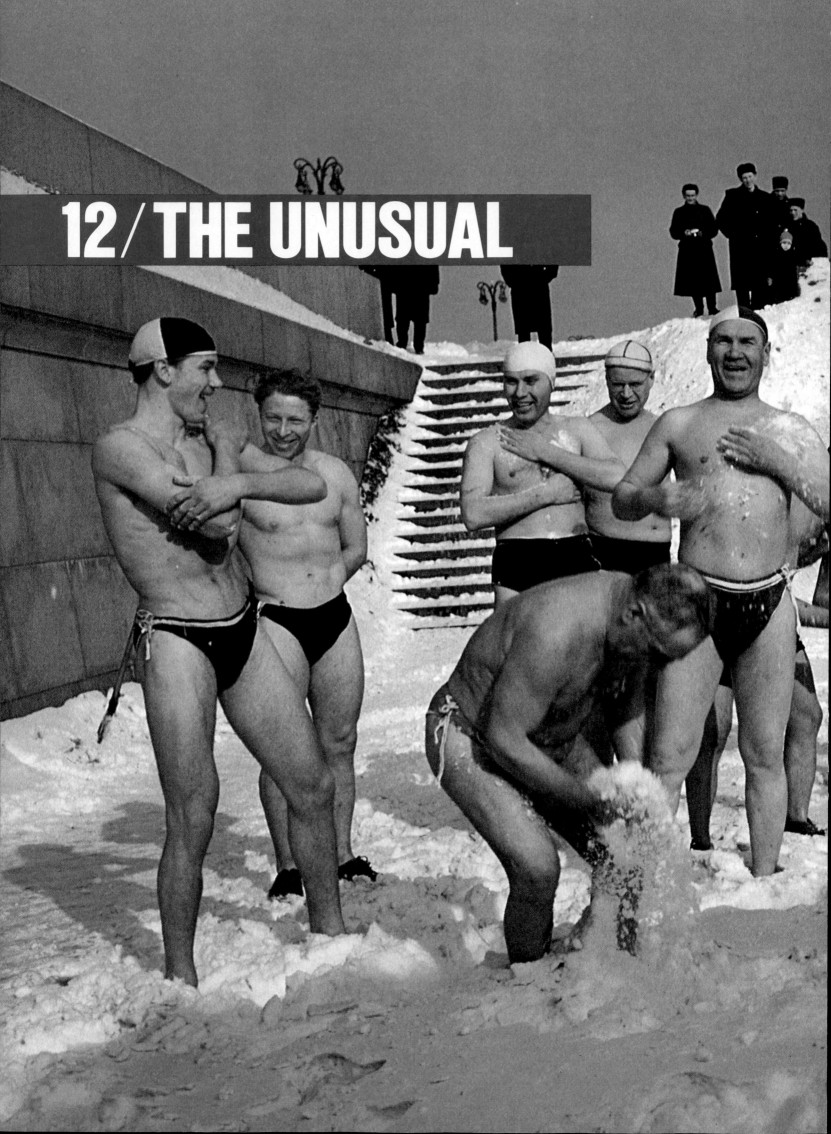

Rubdowns with snow, dips in the icy Moskva River, that's how members of the Moscow polar bear club entertain themselves. They live for *zakal,* a Russian word meaning winter fitness.

"Queen of Racing," she was called. A 65-year-old grandmother, Mrs. Forrest Burright in 1948 spends up to 18 hours a day at Chicago's Maywood Park training and driving the trotters. Having her heart in harness racing for a long time, she explained to *Life,* "I would raise a baby or two, then go back and race some more."

Overcome with joy, probably flabbergasted, a St. Louis Browns' fan vaults straight out of the grandstand at Sportsman's Park in 1944 shortly after his team, ordinarily a cellar dweller, clinched the American League pennant.

A novel way to ski.

A novel way to water ski.

◀ Shooters in York, Pennsylvania, circa 1948.

▼ Johnny Price, who liked to pitch while standing on his head, was signed to a Cleveland Indian contract by Bill Veeck at $10,000 a year in 1946. That was the same Indian team that had Bob Feller, Bob Lemon, and Allie Reynolds already on its pitching staff.

◄ They don't make poles like they used to. Harry Cooper finds that out during the 1948 Olympic trials at Northwestern University's Dyche Stadium. ▼ Easy rider, casual rider, he is in fact participating in a six-day bike race in New York City in 1948, but that does not prevent a few diversions over the long haul, like reading a letter.

► Strange bedfellows, trainer Meshach Tenney shares sleeping quarters at Churchill Downs with his ward Swaps before the 1955 Kentucky Derby. It wasn't just that hotel rooms in Louisville skyrocketed from $8 a night to $30, *Life* reported; Tenney simply preferred it this way.

▼ To celebrate baseball's 100th anniversary in 1939, the St. Louis Cardinals did it with style, employing a tuxedo-clad orchestra known as Rudy Friml Jr.'s Hot Jazz Band.

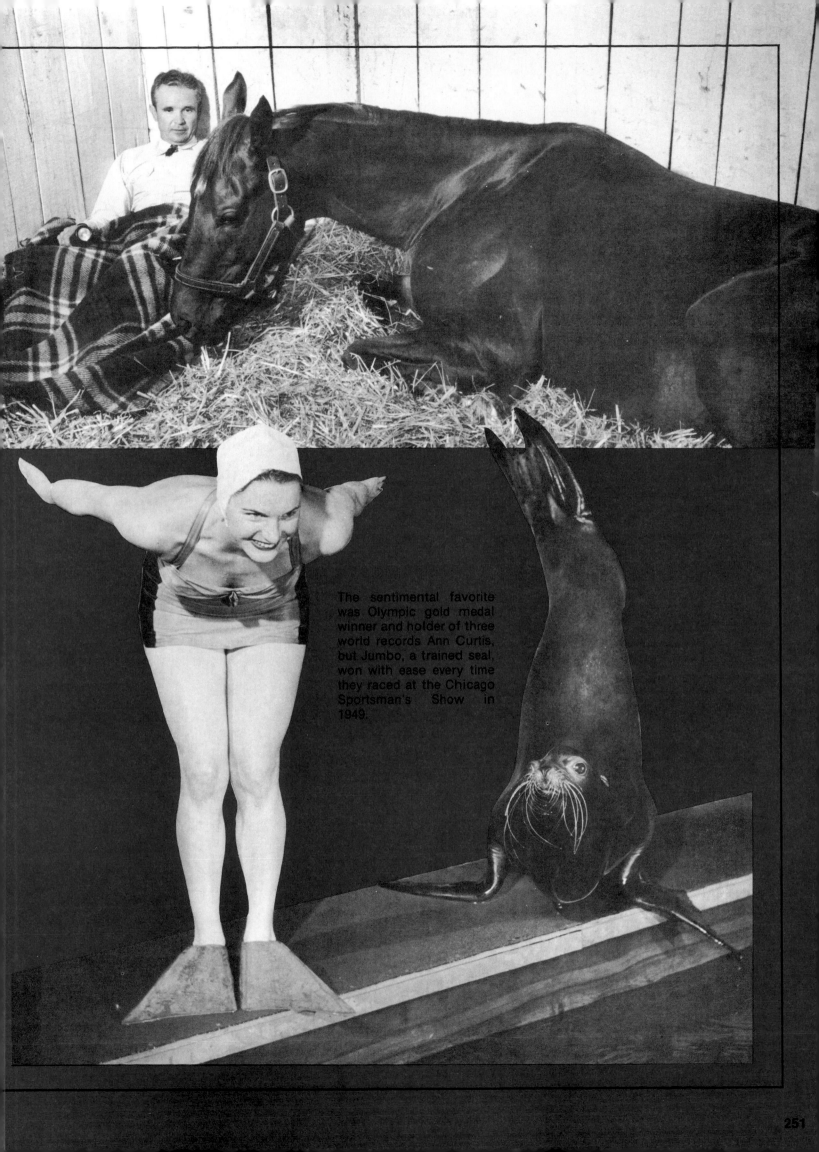

The sentimental favorite was Olympic gold medal winner and holder of three world records Ann Curtis, but Jumbo, a trained seal, won with ease every time they raced at the Chicago Sportsman's Show in 1949.

Going to the prom, surfer-style, in California.

Trout fishing in Japan is a popular pastime. This is opening day of the 1964 trout season along the Kanda River near Tokyo.

Louisiana State coach Paul Dietzel in 1959 told his footballers, "Chinese bandits are the meanest, most vicious characters in the world. From now on, that's what you'll be called." They took him seriously.

Life did a photo essay on 14-year-old diver Kathy Flicker in 1962 but photographer George Silk hardly anticipated getting this shot. *Life* reported, ''Though Kathy Flicker was glad that her stint for the story had ended, no one expected her mind to start wandering. But while she was putting a big swig of water back into the pool at Princeton's Dillon Gym she seemed to lose her head completely . . . a heady example of distortion caused by the water's refraction.''

▲ Gunfighters: in practice and in competition. They come from all walks of life and are dedicated to their sport—commitment such as found here in the Las Vegas hairdresser *(left)* who practices while his client's hair dries; *(right)* Fred Stieler, champion of the national fast-draw tournament.

▼ Who says there isn't some clowning around on a professional baseball field, certainly not Emmett Kelly *(left)* on opening day 1957 at Ebbets Field. He is eavesdropping on whatever it is the umpire is pointing out to Dodger manager Walt Alston (24) and Pittsburgh Pirate shortstop Dick Groat.

PICTURE CREDITS

Sources for the photographs in this book appear below. Credits are grouped by pages and are listed from top to bottom.

1 / CONFRONTATIONS 12–13 Larry Burrows; 14 Larry Burrows (2); 15 Larry Burrows; 16 James Burke, Larry Burrows; 17 UPI/ Bettmann Newsphoto; 18 PIX; 19 Int./UPI/Bettmann Newsphoto, Ed Feeney for *Chicago Tribune* from Associated Press; 20–21 John Zimmerman; 22 Johnny Florea, Int./UPI/Bettmann Newsphoto; 23 Gjon Mili; 24 Hy Peskin, Loomis Dean; 25 Howard Sochurek; 26 Associated Press; 27 Joe Scherschel, Grey Villet; 28 Allan Grant, Frank Scherschel; 29 Herb Scharfman, 30 George Silk; 31 John Shearer.

2 / BASEBALL 32 Ralph Morse; 33 George Strock (2); 34 Loomis Dean, P.I., 35 Loomis Dean, Hy Peskin; 36 Frank & Joe Scherschel, Frank Scherschel; 37 Francis Miller, Frank & Joe Scherschel; 38 Hy Peskin, UPI/Bettmann Newsphoto; 39 Hy Peskin, Ed Clark; 40 Mark Kauffman; 41 Francis Miller, Mark Kauffman; 42 Francis Miller; 43 Loomis Dean; 44 Yale Joel, Francis Miller; 45 Ralph Morse, Yale Joel; 46 George Silk; 47 George Silk; 48–49 Ralph Morse; 50 George Silk (2); 51 George Silk; 52 John Dominis; 53 John Zimmerman; 54 Michael Mauney; 55 John Dominis, Robert Kelley; 56 Francis Miller, Ralph Morse; 57 John Dominis.

3 / IN ACTION 58 John Dominis; 59 Gjon Mili (2); 60 George Silk, John Dominis; 61 Allan Grant, J. R. Eyerman; 62 Yale Joel; 63 George Silk, Francis Miller; 64 Joe Scherschel, Anthony Linck; 65 Mark Kauffman; 66 John Dominis; 67 John Dominis, Thomas McAvoy; 68 Arthur Rickerby; 69 Arthur Rickerby (2); 70 Arthur Rickerby; 71 Peter Stackpole (2); 72 William C. Shrout; 73 George Silk, Richard Meek; 74 Ralph Crane, John Zimmerman; 75 George Silk; 76–77 George Silk; 78 George Silk; 79 John Dominis (4); 80 John Zimmerman; 81 Bill Eppridge (2); 82 Bill Eppridge; 83 Arthur Rickerby.

4 / CELEBRITIES AT SPORT 84 Al P. Burgert; 85 Bill Ray; 86 (left) Crtsy *Life* magazine, Mark Kauffman & Hank Walker; 87 Joe Scherschel, Dmitri Kessel; 88 George Skadding, Stan Wayman; 89 Crtsy *Life* magazine, Co Rentmeester; 90 Stan Wayman, Leonard McCombe; 91 Arthur Schatz; 92 John Dominis; 93 Michael Rougier, Grey Villet (right); 94 Leonard McCombe; 95 Allan Grant (2).

5 / FOOTBALL 96 Bob Doty/Dayton *Journal Herald*; 97 George Strock; 98 Sam Shere, Mark Kauffman; 99 Bob Landry; 100 Al Fenn; 101 John Dominis, Joe Scherschel; 102–103 Ed Clark (top), Mark Kauffman (bottom left), Joe Scherschel (bottom right); 104 Stan Wayman, Francis Miller; 105 George Silk, Paul Schutzer; 106 George Silk (2); 107 George Silk (2); 108 George Silk; 109 George Silk, Arthur Daley; 110 Ralph Morse, Bill Ray; 111 George Silk, Ralph Crane; 112 Bill Eppridge (2); 113 Arthur Rickerby (2); 114 John Zimmerman; 115 Arthur Rickerby; 116 Arthur Rickerby; 117 John Zimmerman; 118 John Zimmerman (2); 119 John Zimmerman.

6 / RACES AND RACERS 120–121 Hank Walker; 122 Gjon Mili, Hank Walker; 123 George Silk; 124 George Silk (2); 125 Arthur Griffin, Gjon Mili; 126 Gjon Mili, Ralph Morse, Wallace Kirkland; 127 Oxford Daily Mail; 128 George Silk; 129 Ralph Morse (2); 130 Arthur Rickerby (left), Leonard McCombe (right), Ralph Morse; 131 George Silk, Bill Eppridge; 132–133 Mark Kauffman; 134 Bill Eppridge, Peter Stackpole; 135 Ralph Crane; 136 Frank & Joe Scherschel, George Silk; 137 Bernard Hoffman & Johnny Florea; 138 Eliot Elisofon, George Silk; 139 Myron Davis.

7 / CUPS, BOWLS, AND OTHER SPORTS CLASSICS 140–141 George Silk; 142 Margaret Bourke-White; 143 George Silk (2); 144 Cornell Capa, Johnny Florea; 145 Mark Kauffman, Peter Stackpole; 146 Mark Kauffman; 147 George Silk; 148 George Silk (2); 149 George Silk; 150–151 Yale Joel (top left), Associated Press (top right), Ralph Morse (bottom left), Grey Villet (bottom right); 152 N. R. Farbman, George Silk; 153 George Silk (2); 154–155 George Silk; 156 Arthur Rickerby; 157 Arthur Rickerby (2); 158 Michael Mauney, George Silk; 159 George Silk, Francis Miller; 160 Joe Scherschel, George Silk; 161 George Silk (2).

8 / GAMES SOME PEOPLE PLAY 162 Gjon Mili; 163 Mark Kauffman; 164–165 George Skadding (top left), Gjon Mili (top right), Mark Kauffman; 166 Dmitri Kessel; 167 Robert W. Kelley, Lee Balterman; 168 Frank Scherschel; 169 Dmitri Kessel; 170 Francis Miller, Leigh Irwin and Nicholas Langen from P.I.; 171 Cornell Capa, Ralph Crane; 172 Arthur Rickerby (2); 173 Arthur Rickerby (2).

9 / BASKETBALL 174 John Zimmerman; 175 David Scherman (left), Myron Davis (right); 176 Edward Clark; 177 Joe Scherschel, Cornell Capa; 178 Ralph Morse, Mark Kauffman and Hank Walker; 179 Ralph Morse; 180 J. R. Eyerman, George Skadding; 181 Hank Walker, Stan Wayman; 182 United Press (left), Ralph Morse (right); 183 John Zimmerman (left), Hy Peskin (right); 184 Bill Ray; 185 Arthur Rickerby (left), John Zimmerman (right); 186 Arthur Rickerby, George Silk; 187 John Zimmerman; 188 John Zimmerman; 189 John Zimmerman (2).

10 / PORTRAITS 190 J. R. Eyerman; 191 Peter Stackpole (top & bottom left), Anthony Linck (right); 192 Bernard Hoffman, Anthony Linck; 193 Anthony Linck, James Burke; 194 Francis Miller; 195 Michael Rougier; 196 Allan Grant, George Skadding; 197 Loomis Dean, Ralph Crane; 198 Grey Villet, Francis Miller; 199 Al Fenn, Cornell Capa; 200 George Silk, Francis Miller; 201 George Silk (top and bottom left), John Dominis (right); 202 Henry Groskinsky; 203 George Silk, Stan Wayman; 204 Loomis Dean; 205 Arthur Rickerby, Ralph Morse; 206 Terence Spencer, John Dominis; 207 Lee Balterman, Arthur Schatz; 208 John Olson, Arthur Rickerby; 209 Co Rentmeester, Michael Mauney; 210 George Silk; 211 John Shearer, John Zimmerman.

11 / THE OLYMPICS 212–213 George Silk; 214 Frank Scherschel; 215 Mark Kauffman (2); 216 Mark Kauffman; 217 Ralph Crane, Mark Kauffman; 218 Don A. Ross; 219 Ralph Crane; 220–221 John Dominis (top left), George Silk (3); 222 Mark Kauffman (2); 223 George Silk (2); 224 George Silk; 225 Larry Burrows, Arthur Rickerby; 226 George Silk; 227 Arthur Rickerby (3); 228 John Dominis from I.O.P.P.; 229 John Dominis from I.O.P.P.; 230 John Dominis; 231 John Dominis (2); 232 John Dominis; 233 John Zimmerman (2); 234 John Zimmerman; 235 Co Rentmeester, Rich Clarkson; 237 Gerald Brimacombe; 238 Heinz Kluetmeier for *Sports Illustrated*; 240–241 Bruce Chambers, Long Beach *Press Telegram*/Gamma Liaison (6); 242 John Zimmerman/LPI; 243 Walter Iooss Jr./Fuji Photo Film U.S.A., Inc.

12 / THE UNUSUAL 244–245 Carl Mydans; 246 Joe Scherschel, Wallace Kirkland; 247 J. R. Eyerman, Mark Kauffman; 248 Bernard Hoffman, Charles Steinheimer; 249 Wallace Kirkland, Ralph Morse; 250 David Scherman; 251 John Dominis, Michael Rougier; 252 Allan Grant, Larry Burrows; 253 George Silk; 254 George Silk; 255 J. R. Eyerman (2), Yale Joel.